Improving School Leadership Through Support, Evaluation, and Incentives

The Pittsburgh Principal Incentive Program

Laura S. Hamilton • *John Engberg* • *Elizabeth D. Steiner*
Catherine Awsumb Nelson • *Kun Yuan*

Sponsored by the Pittsburgh Public Schools

T0308590

RAND EDUCATION

The research in this report was produced within RAND Education, a unit of the RAND Corporation. The research was sponsored by the Pittsburgh Public Schools.

Library of Congress Cataloging-in-Publication Data

Improving school leadership through support, evaluation, and incentives : the Pittsburgh principal incentive program / Laura S. Hamilton ... [et al.].
       p. cm.
   Includes bibliographical references.
   ISBN 978-0-8330-7617-5 (pbk. : alk. paper)
   1. School improvement programs—Pennsylvania—Pittsburgh—Case studies.
   2. Educational leadership—Pennsylvania—Pittsburgh—Case studies. 3. Educational change—Pennsylvania—Pittsburgh—Case studies. 4. School principals—Pennsylvania—Pittsburgh—Case studies. I. Hamilton, Laura S.

LB2822.83.P43I67 2012
371.2'07—dc23
                                                                            2012021169

Cover photograph courtesy iStock

Published 2012 by the RAND Corporation
1776 Main Street, P.O. Box 2138, Santa Monica, CA 90407-2138
1200 South Hayes Street, Arlington, VA 22202-5050
4570 Fifth Avenue, Suite 600, Pittsburgh, PA 15213-2665
RAND URL: http://www.rand.org/
To order RAND documents or to obtain additional information, contact
Distribution Services: Telephone: (310) 451-7002;
Fax: (310) 451-6915; Email: order@rand.org

Preface

In 2007, the Pittsburgh Public Schools (PPS) received funding from the U.S. Department of Education's Teacher Incentive Fund (TIF) program to adopt a set of reforms designed to improve the quality of leadership, including a revised compensation program for principals. The resulting program, the Pittsburgh Urban Leadership System for Excellence (PULSE) initiative, represents a multifaceted approach to improving school leadership and student learning throughout the district. A key component of PULSE is the Pittsburgh Principal Incentive Program (PPIP), a system of performance-based evaluation and compensation through which the district provides principals with support, assistance, and performance-based financial awards tied to measures of their leadership practices and student achievement growth. PULSE and PPIP reflect a growing research-based understanding of the critical role that principal leadership plays in districts' efforts to improve student achievement.

The RAND Corporation partnered with PPS on this grant and played two roles in the project. First, RAND researchers provided advice on the design of the measures used to evaluate principal performance—particularly the measures based on student achievement. Second, RAND served as the project's evaluator. This report addresses the second role, presenting the key findings from the evaluation and discussing their implications for principal evaluation policy and practice. The RAND team provided formative feedback, including specific recommendations for program improvement, directly to PPS through internal memos. This monograph is the final product of the evaluation and focuses on lessons that can be applied to the broader field beyond PPS. It should be of interest to practitioners, policymakers, and researchers designing, implementing, or studying principal evaluation systems.

This research was conducted in RAND Education, a unit of the RAND Corporation. Funding for this work was provided by a subcontract to PPS on the district's TIF grant from the U.S. Department of Education.

For more information about RAND Education, see
http://www.rand.org/education.html

Contents

Figures

Tables

Summary

In 2007, the Pittsburgh Public Schools (PPS) received funding from the U.S. Department of Education's Teacher Incentive Fund (TIF) program to implement the Pittsburgh Urban Leadership System for Excellence (PULSE), a set of reforms designed to improve the quality of school leadership throughout the district. A major component of PULSE is the Pittsburgh Principal Incentive Program (PPIP), a system of support, performance-based evaluation, and compensation. The new compensation system has two major components: (1) an annual opportunity for a permanent salary increase of up to $2,000 based primarily on principals' performance on a rubric that is administered by assistant superintendents (who supervise principals) and that measures practices in several areas and (2) an annual bonus of up to $10,000 based primarily on student achievement growth. The district also offered bonuses to principals who took positions in high-need schools. PPIP provided principals with several forms of support, such as professional development focused on improving leadership, feedback and coaching from assistant superintendents, and participation in Directed Professional Growth (DPG) projects that allowed principals to choose an area in which to work to improve their own skills. The RAND Corporation served as the evaluator of PPIP and examined implementation and outcomes from school years 2007–2008 through 2010–2011. Although the district is likely to continue implementing much of what constitutes PPIP, this report focuses only on the period during which PPIP was being funded by the TIF grant. The evaluation addressed the following broad questions:

- What is the district's theory of action regarding how PPIP is expected to promote improved student outcomes?
- How were the PPIP capacity-building interventions implemented, and how have principals responded to them?
- To what extent have principals' skills and practices changed over the course of PPIP?
- What conditions have changed at the school and classroom levels over the course of PPIP?

- How did principals perform on the rubric and bonus measures, and how was performance related to principal mobility?
- How did student achievement change during the course of PPIP, and how did racial and socioeconomic gaps change?

PPIP is one manifestation of the national focus on improving school leadership as a means of promoting effective teaching and student achievement. PPIP was implemented in a reform-oriented district in which it was one of many ambitious initiatives in place. The most salient addition to the slate of reforms during PPIP's implementation was a district-wide program to improve student achievement and student preparation for postsecondary goals by focusing on improving teacher effectiveness. In 2008–2009, the district developed the Research-Based, Inclusive System of Evaluation (RISE), a new system for observing and evaluating teacher practice and for guiding teacher professional growth. In 2009, based in part on the RISE work, the district received substantial funding from the Bill and Melinda Gates Foundation to implement the Empowering Effective Teachers (EET) program, which incorporated RISE. Many aspects of the EET work were consistent with PPIP. For example, the rubric used to evaluate principals encouraged principals to spend more time in classrooms observing and coaching teachers; the RISE process not only provided the framework for this task but also prompted changes to the principal rubric and to the supports and professional development provided to principals as part of PPIP.

As this discussion illustrates, the designs of EET and PPIP appear to be well aligned, thus providing a context that both supports PPIP implementation and complicates interpretation of the effects of PPIP. In particular, given the context of the district's multiple, overlapping reforms, it is impossible to disentangle any effects of PPIP from the effects of other reforms. Nonetheless, the information presented in this report should contribute to an improved understanding of how reforms like PPIP are implemented, how principals and other school staff respond to these reforms, and what outcomes might be expected to accompany their implementation.

Data and Methods

The evaluation combined qualitative and quantitative data-collection and analysis approaches in an effort to provide a comprehensive understanding of the program theory, implementation, and outcomes. To understand the theory of action guiding the district's design of PPIP and to document the reform's implementation over time, we conducted focus groups and individual interviews with key district staff in all years of the evaluation. We also collected and reviewed extensive documentation, including meeting minutes; documentation of program components, such as the rubric; information about principal professional development; and email exchanges with district staff throughout the four years of the evaluation.

To gain an in-depth understanding of principals' responses to PPIP, changes in principals' practices and skills, and changes in conditions at the school and classroom levels, we conducted interviews and surveys with principals and other school staff. We surveyed principals, online or in-person, during each year of the evaluation. We also surveyed school-level curriculum coaches in years 1, 3, and 4 of the evaluation and teachers in year 4. In addition, we conducted interviews with principals and other school staff in each year of the evaluation. The primary purpose of the interviews was to supplement the surveys by obtaining responses with richer detail and greater depth. To assess principal performance on the rubric and bonus measures, their responses to the high-need school incentive, and changes in student achievement, as well as gaps in achievement, we analyzed administrative data provided by PPS.

Key Findings

What Is the District's Theory of Action Regarding How the Pittsburgh Principal Incentive Program Is Expected to Promote Improved Student Outcomes?

PPIP relied on a combination of capacity-building interventions that included professional development in various forms, evaluation and feedback provided to principals by their supervisors, and financial incentives. District staff viewed the support and feedback interventions as having more potential impact on principal performance than the financial incentives, and principals themselves were more likely to attribute changes in their leadership to support and feedback than to incentives. District leaders posited that the interventions would affect principals by improving principal knowledge and skills and by influencing principals' practices, specifically by increasing time spent on instructional leadership activities. The district also expected PPIP to work by eventually improving the quality of candidates who apply for positions in the district while encouraging less effective principals to leave the district. These changes were then expected to promote learning-focused school environments, improved instruction, and higher levels of student achievement. Our data indicated that the multiple reforms taking place in PPS were perceived as working well together and providing a coherent set of policies focused on raising student achievement throughout the district.

How Were the Pittsburgh Principal Incentive Program Capacity-Building Interventions Implemented, and How Have Principals Responded to Them?

Most principals reported that the PPIP-supported professional development contributed to their professional growth, and, in the final year of the evaluation, principals gave particularly high ratings to learning walks with their internal instructional leadership teams and participation in their own DPG projects. The district provided professional development through the Leadership Academy to promote principals' instructional leadership, and majorities of principals agreed that the Leadership Academy helped them improve their skills across multiple leadership domains, most strongly in the areas of monitoring teachers' instruction and providing feedback to teachers. In addition, nearly two-thirds of principals reported that one-on-one coaching from their assistant superintendents made a moderate or large contribution to their professional growth.

Principals viewed the rubric that was used to evaluate their practices as a useful tool for thinking about their strengths and weaknesses, and we found evidence that principals were increasingly accepting of the idea that unfavorable school conditions should not be considered an excuse for poor performance on this measure. PPS refined the measure over time by reducing the number of standards on the rubric and increasing its focus on principals' roles as instructional leaders and managers of human capital. Principals appreciated these changes and reported that the new rubric standards were well-aligned with the work they were doing to support and evaluate teachers. At the same time, majorities of principals expressed concerns about fairness throughout the course of the evaluation, including a perception that different assistant superintendents used different criteria for assigning ratings and a lack of confidence that the rubric did a good job distinguishing effective from ineffective principals or was fair to all principals regardless of the type of school in which they worked.

Principals' opinions about the bonus measure were mixed; most principals did not report negative effects of the bonus on principal morale or on principals' willingness to collaborate, and fewer than half agreed that "[r]ewarding individual principals based on test score gains is problematic because the principal has limited control over student learning in the school." This finding is noteworthy because it suggests that majorities of principals support the idea that principals are responsible for student learning. However, majorities of principals expressed concerns about the fairness and validity of the specific measures used to award bonuses in PPIP. In particular, principals believed that the likelihood of receiving a bonus was related to student characteristics, even though our analyses suggested no such relationship. The bonus also did not appear to serve as a motivator for most principals; more than two-thirds reported that the prospect of earning a bonus did not affect their practices. In addition, most principals were unaware of the premium for working in high-need schools or did not view it as an incentive to work in those schools. Throughout the evaluation, principals consistently said that money did not motivate them to work harder or to change their practices to raise student achievement and that they therefore found the idea of pay for performance problematic.

To What Extent Have Principals' Skills and Practices Changed over the Course of the Pittsburgh Principal Incentive Program?

Principals reported spending increasing amounts of time observing teachers and providing feedback on their instruction as PPIP matured. Curriculum coaches corroborated these reports of increased principal presence in classrooms and reported that teachers in their schools found principals' feedback useful and that principals were effective in the areas of providing professional development opportunities, giving feedback on instruction, and helping teachers use data. Additional relevant evidence was obtained from a teacher survey in the last year of the evaluation, on which large majorities of teachers rated their principals highly as instructional leaders. Moreover, when principal survey respondents were asked to select areas in which their skills had grown the most since PPIP implementation, the most–frequently selected skills were (1) observing in teachers' classrooms and providing feedback and (2) evaluating teachers.

As noted earlier, the fact that PPS was undertaking multiple reforms makes attribution of any changes directly to PPIP impossible, and this problem of attribution was made more challenging by the fact that the district explicitly tried to ensure that its multiple reforms worked together seamlessly. This coherence among reform efforts was likely beneficial for promoting the desired changes, and the data we collected from principals suggest that principals were hearing the message of a unified approach to reform. In particular, throughout the evaluation, principals who participated in interviews were reluctant to attribute changes in their practice to PPIP, especially to the financial incentives. Instead, principals tended to associate changes in their practice with RISE, and they noted that RISE and PPIP reinforced one another in a way that helped them focus on instructional leadership.

What Conditions Have Changed at the School and Classroom Levels over the Course of the Pittsburgh Principal Incentive Program?

Principals reported becoming more-active users of data for decision making and facilitating such data use among their staffs, and our data from coaches and teachers suggest that principals were providing time, structure, and direct support for instructional data use. Staff at the schools where we conducted interviews reported increased frequency and depth of instructional data use over the four years of PPIP implementation. More generally, majorities of principals and coaches reported seeing specific evidence that three major instructional improvement strategies—principal feedback, site-specific professional development, and use of data—led to specific changes in classrooms. In addition, principals and coaches who participated in interviews in study year 4 described improvements in teaching that included improved questioning techniques, more-effective data use, and increased collaboration among teachers around instruction. Principals and coaches also described increased levels of student engagement—specifically, that students were taking ownership of their own learning, often because the increased data use in the building extended to students and made them more aware of their own progress and where they needed to improve.

How Did Principals Perform on the Rubric and Bonus Measures, and How Was Performance Related to Principal Mobility?

Average principal performance on the rubric remained steady over time, with almost all principals being assigned the highest two out of four categories (proficient or accomplished) on almost all standards on the rubric. On average, principals performed most poorly on the standard related to creating a culture of teaching and learning, which included such activities as data use, curriculum implementation, and differentiated instruction. In interviews, principals said they had made progress on data use, but many said they still struggled with becoming familiar enough with all the curricula their teachers used that they could provide substantive support in that area. Our analysis of the rubric revealed that scores on the individual standards and components were correlated, and the rubric appeared to measure a single construct related to principal leadership. We observed some differences in rubric performance across school type and across schools serving students with different characteristics, although the exact nature of these differences changed from one year to the next.

Performance on the bonus measure was also relatively constant over time and was unrelated to the characteristics of the students in the principal's school. This finding is important because principals expressed concerns that the bonus might favor one type of school (e.g., those serving high-income students) over another, but we saw no evidence of this. This stability in average performance on the bonus measure suggests that an achievement bonus program can be designed so that bonuses change to reflect changes in achievement growth but do not change so much as to create the risk of an overwhelming, unanticipated financial burden. Although the bonus formula was based on absolute rather than relative performance measures, the design process took into consideration prior observed variation in test score gains to limit the risk of very high average bonuses.

We found some evidence that the skills and practices measured by the rubric are associated with improved student achievement. In the final year of the evaluation, mathematics achievement growth showed a statistically significant positive correlation with the first three rubric standards and with the total score. In earlier years, there was evidence of a positive correlation between growth in rubric scores and subsequent achievement growth. Together, these findings provide some evidence that the rubric provided a measure of practices and skills that are associated with principal effectiveness. This relationship is foundational to any program that is trying to improve achievement growth by evaluating and improving practice and should be continually monitored.

Our analysis of mobility showed that the percentage of principals who remained at their schools stayed fairly constant throughout PPIP. Although we did not find significant differences in prior achievement bonuses by move type (i.e., whether the principal left the district, switched schools, retired, or moved for some other reason), the patterns were suggestive. For example, principals who moved into administrative positions at the central office level had higher-than-average achievement bonuses prior to their move than other principals, and those who moved from a principal to an assistant principal position had lower bonuses. This finding is consistent with the hypothesis that high-performing principals would be likely to receive promotions whereas low-performing principals would be counseled into positions that will offer them additional experience to improve their practices. Principals who left the district without retiring had slightly lower achievement than the overall average, a pattern that, if it continues, will lead to a gradual increase in the average performance of principals in PPS. The mobility analysis also showed that principals who moved to higher-need schools had earned higher bonuses than other principals before the move but that high-need schools experienced greater principal turnover than other schools. High levels of turnover may or may not be considered problematic; if the departing principals are replaced by more-effective leaders, turnover could be desirable, at least in the early stages of a reform like PPIP.

How Did Student Achievement Change During the Course of the Pittsburgh Principal Incentive Program, and How Did Racial and Socioeconomic Gaps Change?

Student achievement growth in PPS exceeded that of the rest of the state in three out of four years of PPIP implementation. In year 4, student achievement growth in grades 4–8 in both mathematics and reading reached their highest levels since the beginning of the evaluation. These findings suggest that the implementation of PPIP was accompanied by acceleration in achievement growth, consistent with the district's goal of promoting more-effective school leadership as a means of improving student achievement.

Race and poverty achievement gaps increased over the course of PPIP implementation when measured using scale scores for the same set of students over time. However, there is suggestive evidence that achievement growth among the lowest-scoring students and at the most-disadvantaged schools was beginning to increase. In the final year of the evaluation, previously low-scoring students experienced greater achievement growth than in prior years, which is consistent with a design feature of the bonus formula that rewarded gains at the low end of the distribution more than comparable gains at the high end. Furthermore, we found evidence that achievement growth in high-need schools increased following the implementation of the high-need bonus premium, suggesting that the premium may be promoting increased achievement growth at the most-disadvantaged schools. These findings suggest that PPIP can be an important part of the district's efforts to reduce the achievement gap.

Recommendations

The findings presented in this report do not provide definitive evidence regarding the effects of performance-based evaluation and compensation for principals, so they do not support recommendations regarding whether or not districts or states should adopt such policies. Nonetheless, these findings are potentially useful not only for helping PPS as it continues to implement its ambitious reform agenda but also for informing other districts, states, charter management organizations, and other education agencies that are developing new principal evaluation and compensation systems. We provide several recommendations that PPS and other entities might consider as they develop or revise principal evaluation, support, and compensation policies.

Recommendations for Evaluation System and Measure Development

Consider incorporating a range of measures into the evaluation system, including measures that reflect input from a variety of stakeholders. Teachers, coaches, and other school staff can provide an important perspective on principals' leadership quality and can be useful for helping districts understand whether principals' instructional improvement efforts are leading to the desired effects on schools. Information from other stakeholders, such as parents and students, could also prove helpful for understanding principals' performance. These data could be collected in a variety of ways but, for the purposes of formal evaluation, should be collected consistently across schools and ideally in a way that permits quantification of the information. It is critical that any measure used for the purpose of evaluating principals be carefully piloted and subject to an investigation of the validity of that measure for that specific purpose; instruments that work well for providing formative feedback, for instance, could provide misleading information or be subject to score corruption if used for high-stakes evaluation purposes.

Gather evidence of validity, reliability, and fairness of the system throughout the implementation of the system, not just at the beginning. The changes we observed in the correlations between the bonus and rubric measures illustrate how the characteristics of scores can change over time. Districts should continually gather evidence to identify changes in rater agreement, relationships among measures, relationships with external criteria, and fairness to all participants. Alignment of the system with broader district or state goals should be a focus of these ongoing investigations.

Take steps to ensure consistency in application of rubrics across evaluators. Principals need assurance that the method used to assign ratings is fair to all principals, regardless of what type of school they lead or who their evaluator happens to be. Although traditional methods for measuring interrater agreement are difficult to apply in some systems (e.g., in PPIP, each rater works with only a certain type of school, so it is difficult to obtain multiple ratings for one principal), other approaches could help promote consistency. These include calibration meetings at which the evaluators rate evidence and discuss their rating criteria, comparisons of the distributions of scores produced by each evaluator to help them identify the extent to which their ratings differ in magnitude or in variability, and examination of the narrative comments that evaluators produce. Regardless of the approach taken, the district or state adopting the evaluation system should let principals know that it is taking steps to improve consistency of evaluation and should provide professional development to raters to promote high-quality evaluation.

On measures of principal practice, develop a scale that differentiates performance at all points along the distribution. Because the vast majority of scores assigned to principals were high, the four-point rating scale used in PPIP offered little opportunity to distinguish between the most-outstanding principals and those who are performing well but not at the highest level. Developing a more expansive rating scale that permits fine-grained distinctions at the high end of the distribution could help districts and states ensure that they are encouraging and rewarding the most-effective principals and could provide information that is useful for identifying principals who could serve in mentoring roles. It could also support targeted professional development for principals. One way to expand the rating scale is to award higher scores to principals who not only perform well themselves but who also help promote the skills and knowledge of others with whom they work.

Involve all stakeholders in any reviews and redesigns of measures used in evaluation systems. Incentive pay systems designed to reward complex changes in behavior are, by definition, complicated and often controversial. It is important that districts cultivate shared goals among stakeholders, such as parents, teachers, principals, and central office staff. Once shared goals are established, measures can be reviewed based on their ability to attain these goals.

Monitor racial and socioeconomic achievement gaps using student-level growth throughout the achievement distribution. Given the importance that many districts have placed on the goal of reducing achievement gaps, it would be worthwhile to monitor progress toward this goal using multiple metrics. The practice of tracking changes in percentage proficient across cohorts provides useful information, but it may lead to distorted impressions regarding the nature and extent of improvement among individual students who are performing at different points in the achievement distribution. By also examining student-level growth in scale scores for students who remain in a district for at least two consecutive years, the district could provide richer and more-accurate information to inform its own decision making and to enhance public understanding of the district's progress.

Recommendations for Implementation

Align the elements of a performance-based compensation system, including support and criteria for evaluation, with the district's approach to improving teaching and learning. Principals who are participating in multiple, simultaneous reforms are more likely to support the reforms and respond effectively when the reforms are well connected and aligned with a common set of goals. Districts undertaking reforms like PPIP should consider the extent to which evaluation criteria, professional development, and other elements of the reform support or conflict with other key initiatives.

Devise a communication strategy that provides clear, timely, and ongoing information to help principals understand the evaluation measures and the steps the district took to ensure their validity. Principals' concerns and lack of understanding of some aspects of PPIP suggest that any effort by a district or other entity to adopt performance-based compensation should be accompanied not only by efforts to establish the validity and reliability of the measures but also by a communication strategy that provides clear, timely, and ongoing information to stakeholders. A comprehensive communication strategy should involve multiple vehicles of communication, including large-group meetings, as well as individualized interactions and stakeholder involvement in decisions about changes to the program.

Provide principals with concrete tools for accomplishing the instructional leadership tasks (especially observing and providing feedback on instruction) encouraged by the compensation system. In PPIP, such resources as professional development, targeted support from supervisors, and a clear set of standards communicated by the rubric, were perceived by principals as contributing to their professional growth. The positive perceptions about the utility of the DPG projects suggest that this type of activity could be a valuable tool, particularly for helping more-experienced and more-accomplished principals enhance their knowledge and skills in a particular area.

Help principals find the time needed to engage in the practices promoted by the initiative. If the initiative encourages principals to spend more time on specific tasks, such as supporting teachers, it is important to help them find that time. Districts could encourage discussion of tasks on which principals might spend less time and the most-effective ways to incorporate delegation in their leadership approach. Districts could also create structures that facilitate delegation. The ability to cultivate leadership among school staff is an important element of effective leadership and could be directly incorporated into the evaluation and support systems, particularly for experienced principals.

Assess the extent to which principal mobility leads to improved access to effective principals at high-need schools and to higher levels of principal effectiveness overall. We found that high-need schools experienced greater principal mobility than other schools, but also that principals who switched schools and moved to higher-need schools had higher prior performance on the bonus measure than those who moved to lower-need schools. It is not clear whether the higher mobility levels in high-need schools will lead to disruption or to improved educational quality, so districts and states should monitor mobility over time to determine whether equity and overall effectiveness are improving.

Conclusion

The implementation of PPIP during the period of the TIF grant was accompanied by changes in the practices, skills, and attitudes of principals and other school and district staff. Each year, the district modified elements of the program in response to challenges it encountered. The district's experiences can be informative for efforts to establish new evaluation and compensation systems for principals in other districts or in states, charter management organizations, or other education agencies. Some of the recommendations presented in this summary stem from the unique context in which PPIP was operating, but most of them are likely to be applicable to some degree in other contexts and can serve as a resource for future principal evaluation reforms.

Acknowledgments

Many individuals contributed to this monograph. We thank all the current and former staff at PPS for their support throughout this evaluation, particularly superintendent Linda Lane, Alyssa Ford-Heywood, Jeannine French, Lorraine Marnet, Christiana Otuwa, Jay Pan, Paulette Poncelet, and Barbara Rudiak. We are also indebted to the many administrators, principals, coaches, teachers, and other school staff who participated in the study and shared their valuable time and insights with us.

The project would not have been completed without the assistance of our colleagues from RAND, including Amalavoyal Chari, Robert Hickam, Stephanie Lonsinger, Andrea Phillips, Rena Rudavsky, and Shannah Tharp-Taylor. We are also grateful to Brian Gill at Mathematica Policy Research, who contributed to the design of the bonus measures and the evaluation plan, and to Deborah Holtzman at the American Institutes for Research, who led the teacher survey effort for the Intensive Partnership Sites evaluation (funded by the Bill and Melinda Gates Foundation). We thank Catherine Augustine, Cathy Stasz, Brian Stecher, and Ron Zimmer for their thoughtful reviews and comments on earlier versions of this monograph, Lisa Bernard for her skillful editing, and Steve Oshiro for his assistance with production.

The study was funded by a subcontract to the Pittsburgh Public Schools, which received funds to implement the Pittsburgh Principal Incentive Program from the U.S. Department of Education's Teacher Incentive Fund program.

Abbreviations

AERA	American Educational Research Association
ALA	Accelerated Learning Academy
ANOVA	analysis of variance
APA	American Psychological Association
AYP	Adequate Yearly Progress
CIPP	context, input, process, and product
DIBELS	Dynamic Indicators of Basic Early Literacy Skills
DPG	Directed Professional Growth
EET	Empowering Effective Teachers
EFA	Excellence for All
ELA	English language arts
ETS	Educational Testing Service
FPL	federal poverty level
FRL	free or reduced-price lunch
IEP	individualized education program
ISLLC	Interstate School Leaders Licensure Consortium
ITL	instructional teacher leader
LEP	limited English proficiency
NCLB	No Child Left Behind
NCME	National Council on Measurement in Education

PAIA	Pittsburgh Administrator Induction Academy
PELA	Pittsburgh Emerging Leaders Academy
PFT	Pittsburgh Federation of Teachers
Pittsburgh CAPA	Pittsburgh High School for the Creative and Performing Arts
PPIP	Pittsburgh Principal Incentive Program
PPS	Pittsburgh Public Schools
PSSA	Pennsylvania System of School Assessment
PULSE	Pittsburgh Urban Leadership System for Excellence
RISE	Research-Based, Inclusive System of Evaluation
RTI	Real Time Information
SPI-2	School Performance Index 2
TIF	Teacher Incentive Fund
TLT	Teaching and Learning Team
TOA	theory of action
UPMC	University of Pittsburgh Medical Center
VAL-ED	Vanderbilt Assessment of Leadership in Education
VAM	value-added measure

CHAPTER ONE

Introduction

The quality of leadership provided by a school's principal is widely regarded as an important contributor to the quality of teaching and learning in the school (Hallinger and Heck, 1996; Knapp et al., 2003; Leithwood et al., 2004; Lachat and Smith, 2005; Darling-Hammond et al., 2007; Grissom and Loeb, 2009). As school districts across the United States seek to improve the performance of their schools, the preparation and effectiveness of principals are key considerations, and states and districts have adopted policies that are intended to improve principal recruitment, professional development, and evaluation (Augustine et al., 2009). These efforts accelerated in response to federal initiatives, such as Race to the Top, which incentivized states to undertake certain reforms, including revamping teacher and principal evaluation systems.

In 2007, the Pittsburgh Public Schools (PPS) received funding from the U.S. Department of Education's Teacher Incentive Fund (TIF) program to adopt a set of reforms designed to improve the quality of leadership provided by the district's principals. The resulting program, the Pittsburgh Urban Leadership System for Excellence (PULSE) initiative, represents a multifaceted approach to improving school leadership and student learning throughout the district.[1] A key component of PULSE is the Pittsburgh Principal Incentive Program (PPIP), a system of evaluation and performance-based compensation through which the district provides principals with support, assistance, and performance-based financial awards tied to measures of practices and student achievement growth. PULSE and PPIP reflect a growing research-based understanding of the critical role that principal leadership plays in districts' efforts to improve student achievement.

PPIP includes a set of capacity-building interventions that are intended to improve student achievement through a causal pathway that starts with the improvement of the quality of instructional leadership provided by principals. These capacity-building interventions include professional development to improve leadership, evaluation and

---

[1] PULSE is a leadership development program that consists of six core components: the Pittsburgh Emerging Leaders Academy (PELA), the new administrator's induction program, Leadership Academy for principals, assistant superintendent training and mentoring, performance-based evaluation, and performance-based compensation. At the district's request, we focus on the last two components, which comprise PPIP.

feedback, and incentives, each of which is described in detail in Chapter Three, along with the proposed causal pathways through which the district expected these interventions to improve student outcomes.

PPIP includes several measures that are used to award performance-based compensation to principals. The first is the Administrators' Performance Standard Rubric (hereafter referred to as *the rubric*), which includes a set of standards, each with several components, on which principals were rated by their supervisors (called assistant superintendents) across four levels of performance: rudimentary, emerging, proficient, and accomplished.[2] These ratings draw on evidence that the principal assembles, as well as evidence that the assistant superintendent gathers through interactions and observations. Assistant superintendents are expected to meet individually with principals as part of their evaluation and to provide specific feedback to guide improvement and suggestions for professional development. Performance on the rubric determines, in part, the amount of the salary increment of up to $2,000 that is permanently added to each principal's base salary. The amount of the increment depends on a principal's performance on the evaluation rubric, his or her tenure as a PPS principal, and the Adequate Yearly Progress (AYP) status of his or her school. Most principals are evaluated every three years, though newer principals are evaluated more often, as discussed in Chapter Three. Those who are not evaluated in a given year participate in a Directed Professional Growth (DPG) project that determines, along with AYP status and principal tenure, the annual salary increment (see Chapter Three for details).

The other new component of principals' compensation under PPIP is an annual bonus of up to $10,000. The bonus amount is based on the performance of the principal's school on the achievement measures in a given school year and, starting in year 3 of PPIP implementation, the high-need status of his or her school. The bonus is based on a set of student achievement measures and, in schools serving grades 9 through 12, a set of additional measures, including improvements in college-level course participation and performance (grades 11 and 12), SAT® exam participation (grade 12), and the percentages of students "on track" to graduate (the on-track measure, which captures overall credit completion in grades 9 through 12). These high school measures are included in the bonus calculation for any principal whose school contains one or more of those grades. Together, the rubric and bonus measures form the basis of a performance-based compensation system that is intended to incentivize effective practice and improved student outcomes.

---

[2]   During the implementation of PPIP, the district had five assistant superintendents in years 1–3 and four assistant superintendents in year 4, each of whom supervised principals at a particular type of school (i.e., K–5, high school, or special school).

What We Know About Relationships Between School Leadership and Student Achievement

In designing the components of PPIP, district leaders drew on research indicating that the quality of a principal's leadership is positively related to achievement gains among students in the school (Rice, 2010). In 2004, Leithwood and colleagues published a review that synthesized findings from a large number of studies examining the relationship between principals and student achievement. These authors identified school leadership as the second-most important contributor to student achievement, after classroom instruction, and they found that the relationship between leadership and achievement was strongest in low-performing schools. More recently, Louis and colleagues (2010) completed a review that provides additional support for the claim that principal leadership is the second-most important school-based factor contributing to student achievement, after instruction. These authors point out that principals have responsibility for a large number of school practices and conditions, each of which alone might make a small contribution to achievement but that, together, could exert a substantial effect.

Despite this large and growing body of evidence, it is challenging to disentangle the effect of the principal from other effects, including those exerted by teachers, and most of the existing studies do not support causal conclusions about principals' effectiveness. One study that does provide strong evidence of principals' direct influence on achievement is an analysis of Texas data by Branch, Hanushek, and Rivkin (2012). These authors use a value-added modeling approach with principal and school fixed effects, as well as controls for principal transitions to isolate the effect of the principal from other factors, such as teacher effects. Their analysis suggests that principals do matter and that their effectiveness at raising student achievement varies substantially, particularly in high-poverty schools.

Although the literature suggests that principals contribute to student outcomes, identifying the specific characteristics and practices that enable principals to raise student achievement has been challenging. Principals play a variety of roles within their schools, including instructional, managerial, and political roles (Cuban, 1988). The Wallace Foundation has identified five key functions that principals must perform well in order to be effective: shaping a vision of academic success for all students, creating a climate hospitable to education, cultivating leadership in others, improving instruction, and managing people, data, and processes to foster school improvement (Wallace Foundation, 2012). The ways in which principals allocate their time within and across these functions are likely to influence their effectiveness. A 2003 research synthesis conducted by researchers at Mid-Continent Research for Education and Learning (Waters, Marzano, and McNulty, 2003) identified 21 leadership responsibilities that have been associated with improved student achievement in prior studies. Some of these responsibilities address instruction directly, whereas others (e.g., establishing standard operating procedures and routines) pertain more to the management of the school environment. The quality of the studies included in the review is mixed, however, and the findings are far from definitive, so it is difficult to say with confidence which of the specific responsibilities matters most.

The category of leadership activities that has arguably received the most attention in recent years is the set of actions that are typically described as instructional leadership (Robinson, Lloyd, and Rowe, 2008). Researchers have used a variety of definitions of *instructional leadership*, but one commonly used conceptualization was put forth by Hallinger and Murphy (1985), who describe three dimensions: defining the school's mission, managing the instructional program, and promoting a positive school learning climate. This work involves not only direct interactions with teachers in the classroom but also efforts to influence the organization of the school and to interact with external constituents who can support the learning goals of the school (Knapp, Copland, and Talbert, 2003; Leithwood et al., 2004). In fact, direct supervision of classroom teaching is not one of the factors that consumes the bulk of most principals' time, particularly in middle and high schools (Hallinger and Heck, 1996); instead, principals tend to exert influence on instruction by shaping the school's culture and climate and providing opportunities for collaboration and professional development (Hallinger, 2005; Supovitz, Sirinides, and May, 2010). Moreover, principals' allocation of time, as well as their effectiveness, is often related to their ability and opportunities to distribute leadership responsibilities among a leadership team within the school. However, even in schools with shared leadership, the principal's role remains critical to improving educational outcomes (Fullan, 2006; Heck and Hallinger, 2009).

There is limited research that directly examines how principals spend their time and how this allocation of time relates to student outcomes. A study by Horng, Klasik, and Loeb (2010) involved gathering direct observations of principals' time allocation across six categories of tasks: administration, organization management, day-to-day instruction, instructional program, internal relations, and external relations. In an analysis that related time spent on each of these categories to gains in student achievement, the only significant predictor of achievement gains was time spent on organizational management activities, such as hiring and managing staff and managing budgets. In contrast, time spent on instructional leadership was not associated with gains in achievement. Time spent on organizational management was also positively associated with teachers' perceptions of the quality of the school environment. The value-added analysis by Branch, Hanushek, and Rivkin (2012) provides additional support for the importance of organizational management. That study suggests that one of the mechanisms through which principals influence achievement is through their management of teacher turnover, with more-effective principals being more likely than other principals to have their least effective teachers leave the school.

Other research indicates that teachers' perceptions of working conditions, including the quality of school leadership, influence teacher turnover (Ladd, 2009) and that a principal's effectiveness at improving achievement is associated with his or her likelihood of attracting, motivating, and retaining effective teachers (Beteille, Kalogrides, and Loeb, 2009; Fuller, Young, and Baker, 2011). Hallinger, Bickman, and Davis (1996) found that principals' contributions to student learning gains occurred through their efforts to improve the school climate. Similarly, a study by Supovitz, Sirinides, and May (2010) found that principals promote improved student learning in large part through their influence on teachers' practices and on teachers' opportunities to communicate and collaborate with one another. Together, these findings point to the importance of understanding how principals interact with teachers and how teachers respond to a principal's leadership.

Two additional important considerations involve principal retention and the distribution of effective principals across schools. On the topic of retention, Branch, Hanushek, and Rivkin (2012) found that principals who received the lowest scores on their value-added achievement measure were more likely than other principals to leave their schools, but most of these principals became principals in other schools rather than leaving the profession. If these principals are moving to schools in which they are more effective, either because of a better match between the principal's skills and school context or because the principal improved his or her skills over time, the finding that these least effective principals continue to lead schools might not be of concern. To date, however, there is no evidence that they do improve. These authors also find that the most-effective principals are more likely to remain in their schools than the least effective, but less likely than the principals who perform near the middle of the effectiveness distribution. Principal retention is important because experience leading a particular school has been shown to be positively associated with effectiveness at improving student outcomes (Coelli and Green, 2012).

The way in which principals are distributed across schools is also likely to influence student outcomes, and it is relevant to the topic of retention because schools serving the most-disadvantaged students are more likely than other schools to be led by principals who score low on measures of effectiveness or on characteristics associated with effectiveness, such as years of experience (Grissom and Loeb, 2009; Horng, Kalogrides, and Loeb, 2009; Rice, 2010). In particular, disadvantaged schools tend to experience higher levels of principal turnover than lower-need schools do (Burkhauser et al., 2012). However, some research indicates that effective principals are likely to remain in their schools even if those schools serve low-income or low-achieving students (Branch, Hanushek, and Rivkin, 2012), which suggests that policies focused on attracting effective principals to high-need schools may pay off by enabling those schools to acquire and keep good principals.

The Need for New Systems for Evaluating Principals

The growing body of literature on the importance of principals, combined with an interest in rethinking accountability and compensation for schools and school staff, has led to a rapid rise in the development of systems for evaluating principals' performance, and many of these systems have been designed to recognize principals' roles as instructional leaders (Hallinger, 2005). Recent reviews (Goldring et al., 2009; Davis, Kearney, et al., 2011) of principal evaluation systems, however, have revealed some problems with existing approaches to evaluating principals. These include lack of evidence of technical quality of the measures and inadequate attention to principals' work in the areas of curriculum and instruction (Goldring et al., 2009), as well as lack of fidelity of implementation of systems to the rubrics and guidelines that are intended to inform implementation (Davis, Kearney, et al., 2011). One system that has demonstrated evidence of good technical quality and that has been implemented widely is the Vanderbilt Assessment of Leadership in Education (VAL-ED) evaluation tool (Porter et al., 2010), which involves gathering data from school staff, as well as principals' supervisors, and which is based on a conceptual framework that links core components of learning-centered leadership with key processes, such as planning, supporting, and monitoring.

Although the research base on what factors influence the effectiveness of principal evaluations is thin, several scholars have provided guidance on factors that are likely to promote good evaluation practice. One of the most-important considerations is the linking of evaluation to a set of clear standards for performance that can be easily understood by principals (Goldring et al., 2009; Derrington and Sanders, 2011). A study by Kimball, Milanowski, and McKinney (2009) highlights the potential value, but also the limits, of evaluation systems linked to clear standards. These authors found that principals who were randomly assigned to a standards-based evaluation system had more-positive impressions of the evaluation system than principals who remained in their district's non–standards-based system but that these impressions were negatively affected by inadequate fidelity to the specified procedures and criteria within the standards-based group. This finding raises another important consideration, which is the need to ensure that those who conduct evaluations are trained to follow the procedures and to apply the evaluation criteria with high levels of accuracy and consistency. Along similar lines, the relationship between the supervisor or evaluator and the principal is one potential influence on the quality and utility of the evaluations and is most likely to promote effective evaluation when it is characterized by mutual trust (West and Derrington, 2009).

Of course, one of the most-important factors in the design of a principal evaluation system is the quality and breadth of measures included. There is widespread agreement within the measurement community that evaluations that are used for high-stakes purposes should rely on multiple sources of evidence and that each source should be assessed in terms of its ability to produce information that is valid for the intended purposes of the evaluation (American Educational Research Association [AERA], American Psychological Association [APA], and National Council on Measurement in Education [NCME], 1999). Most existing systems rely on composite measures that include both student achievement and principals' practices (Lipscomb et al., 2010). The VAL-ED system incorporates evidence from several sources, including supervisor ratings, teacher ratings, and documentation that accompanies those ratings (Porter et al., 2010). However, although multiple-measure systems are becoming increasingly common, few of these systems (one exception is the VAL-ED) have been subjected to the reliability and validity investigations that would be needed to understand the relationships among the components and the extent to which the components, separately and together, provide evidence of effective leadership (Davis, Kearney, et al., 2011).

Another potentially important consideration in the design of evaluation systems is the role of professional development. Research suggests that high-quality professional development for principals should emphasize the variety of roles principals play in their schools and should provide principals with opportunities to apply what they learn in realistic settings and to work with mentors (Davis, Darling-Hammond, et al., 2005). It should also be ongoing, offering learning opportunities throughout a principal's career, and should address principals' specific needs (Peterson, 2002). Much of the existing professional development offered to principals is viewed as weak on these criteria (Portin et al., 2003). By linking evaluation to well-designed and customized professional development, districts could promote a system that offers principals learning opportunities that are clearly aligned with their strengths and weaknesses as identified in the evaluation.

There is evidence that good evaluation can promote desired principal behaviors. A study by Sun and Youngs (2009) examined relationships between evaluation and principals' practices in 13 Michigan school districts and found that principals in districts that used evaluations to hold principals accountable were more likely than other principals to engage in practices related to student learning, such as supporting instruction. Those authors also observed relationships between the content of the evaluations and principals' practices, with principals who were evaluated based on behaviors relevant to learning showing a greater tendency to emphasize those behaviors in their practice than principals who were evaluated based on other criteria.

Evaluation and feedback might be particularly valuable during a principal's early years in his or her school. Principal experience is a significant predictor of principals' effectiveness at improving school performance (Clark, Martorell, and Rockoff, 2009), and low-achieving schools are more likely than other schools to be led by principals with limited experience (Branch, Hanushek, and Rivkin, 2012). To the extent that evaluations can serve as a tool to promote practices that are most likely to improve student learning, new principals might be especially likely to benefit from high-quality evaluation.

Taken together, the studies reviewed in this chapter suggest that principals have an important role to play in promoting school improvement, but the evidence regarding the specific principal characteristics or practices that are associated with student achievement and other outcomes is not conclusive. Moreover, high-quality evaluation is likely to contribute to principal quality, but we do not yet know the specific features of evaluations that are likely to be most effective. Efforts to improve principal support and evaluation policies should be subject to scrutiny, both to help those states or districts adjust their policies to make them work better and to inform the broader field about what seems to work well and what steps might improve the implementation and outcomes associated with these policies.

Evaluation Questions

Informed by a research-based understanding of the importance of principals and the role that high-quality principal evaluation can play in promoting improved student learning, PPS district leaders designed PPIP to incorporate features that have been suggested to be important components of high-quality evaluation. Most notably, PPIP used multiple measures, linked evaluation to professional development, and was intended to foster a culture of continuous feedback and learning. The RAND evaluation was designed to examine the implementation of PPIP over the course of the district's TIF grant, providing formative feedback to the district each year to guide the district's decision making about program design and implementation. We provided internal reports and briefings to the district to support this goal. The evaluation was also intended to provide a final, summative perspective on how PPIP was being implemented at the end of the district's TIF grant, how principals and other staff had responded to it, and how student outcomes were affected by the program. This report summarizes findings from the summative portion of the evaluation, addressing the following questions:

- What is the district's theory of action (TOA) regarding how PPIP is expected to promote improved student outcomes?
- How were the PPIP capacity-building interventions implemented, and how have principals responded to them?
- In what ways did principals' skills and practices change over the course of PPIP?
- What conditions changed at the school and classroom levels over the course of PPIP?
- How did principals perform on the rubric and bonus measures, and how was performance related to principal mobility?
- How did student achievement change during the course of PPIP, and how did racial and socioeconomic gaps change?

Although the district is likely to continue implementing much of what constitutes PPIP, this report focuses only on the period during which PPIP was being funded by the TIF grant. It is important to recognize that we cannot answer what is arguably the most important question about PPIP, which is whether the implementation of the program resulted in improved student learning. As we discuss later in this report, PPS enacted a wide variety of reforms over the course of the PPIP initiative, and it is impossible to disentangle any effects of PPIP from the effects of these other reforms. Moreover, the PPIP interventions and incentives were applied district-wide, so there is no nonparticipating control group with which to compare the outcomes experienced by PPIP participants. Nonetheless, the information presented in this report should contribute to an improved understanding of how compensation-based reforms like PPIP are implemented in practice, how principals respond to these reforms, and what outcomes might be likely to accompany their implementation.

Organization of This Report

Chapter Two describes our general approach to evaluating PPIP, as well as the data sources and methods used in the evaluation. In Chapter Three, we discuss the broader district context in which PPIP was implemented and present the TOA that guided our evaluation (evaluation question 1). Findings related to principals' reactions to the PPIP interventions (evaluation question 2) appear in Chapter Four, and findings related to changes in principals' skills and actions (evaluation question 3), as well as changes in their schools and classrooms (evaluation question 4) are presented in Chapter Five. In Chapter Six, we present results of analyses of principal performance on the rubric and bonus measures, as well as analyses of principal mobility and its relationship to principal performance on these measures (evaluation question 5). Chapter Seven presents the findings related to changes in overall student achievement and in achievement gaps within the district (evaluation question 6). The report concludes with a brief summary of findings and discusses their implications for policy and practice. Appendixes with supporting data are published separately and available for download.

CHAPTER TWO

Data Sources and Analytic Approach

The evaluation is organized around a TOA that depicts the PPIP interventions, the intended outcomes, and the mechanisms through which the interventions are expected to influence the outcomes. We worked with district staff to clarify the interventions, intended outcomes, and mechanisms and used this information to develop the TOA, which is described in detail in Chapter Three. There are several benefits to using a TOA to frame the evaluation:

- PPIP was one of the few TIF grants in the 2006–2007 funding round that focused on performance-based compensation for principals, and it has attracted attention from local and national media as a potential model for reshaping how school leaders are supported and rewarded. Other urban school systems could benefit from evidence regarding *how* the program works, in addition to whether it works as a means of promoting improved student achievement.
- The evaluation was intended to serve both formative and summative purposes, helping the district understand the program's strengths and weaknesses and providing guidance for improving its implementation. Establishing and testing a clear framework for PPIP's interventions and intended outcomes provided a structure for targeted improvements as the program matured.
- Presenting findings within the context of the district's TOA allows us to identify challenges to implementation and to consider how they might be addressed in a manner consistent with the overall logic and goals of the program.

This approach is intended to align with the context, input, process, and product (CIPP) model of evaluation. The CIPP model, originally proposed by Daniel Stufflebeam more than 40 years ago (Stufflebeam, 1966), is intended to help make evaluation findings useful for program improvement rather than simply providing summative judgments of program effectiveness. The model is now in its fifth installment (Stufflebeam, 2000).

The four letters in the CIPP abbreviation stand for

- context: What needs to be done? What is the issue to be addressed or problem to be solved?
- input: How should it be done? What resources or strategies will be applied to the problem?
- process: Is it being done? Are the inputs being implemented as intended?
- product: Did it succeed? Did the inputs as implemented achieve the desired result?

The TOA analysis provides discussion of the *context* in which PPIP is being implemented and the *inputs* the district intends to develop. The collection of evidence regarding the implementation of each TOA element supports an evaluation of the *process* of implementation, and the analysis of outcomes provides information about the program's success (i.e., a *product* evaluation). This approach is also consistent with theory-based evaluation (Weiss, 1997; Birckmayer and Weiss, 2000), which approaches program evaluation through the identification and testing of assumptions on which the program is based, including the assumptions regarding the mechanisms through which program activities are hoped to lead to the desired outcomes.

Data Sources

The evaluation combines qualitative and quantitative data-collection and analysis approaches in an effort to provide a comprehensive understanding of the program theory and implementation, as well as an exploration of program outcomes. It includes data from a variety of sources, including documentation and district administrative data, as well as primary data collected from district- and school-level staff. The inclusion of multiple data sources is intended to help illuminate the district's TOA and to help us understand the ways in which principals and other groups have responded to the PPIP interventions. We describe each of the data sources in this section. Although we discuss the data gathered during each year of the evaluation, the bulk of the findings reported in later chapters rely on the most recent round of data collection because the primary purpose of this report is to document the status of PPIP at the end of the district's TIF grant.

Principal Surveys

We surveyed principals in the spring each year starting in the 2007–2008 school year, with the final administration taking place in spring 2011. We drew many of the survey items from existing instruments, including surveys developed for RAND's National Center on Performance Incentives and comprehensive school reform evaluations, and modified the instruments in response to written comments from district staff. Items that had not been validated in other surveys were piloted with a small number of principals, and we modified the items as necessary to address concerns about clarity or meaning. The principal survey included questions on principals' time allocation across various tasks, participation in and satisfaction with formal and informal professional development, their interactions with their assistant superintendents, conditions in their schools, their opinions about PPIP and its incentives, leadership activities, confidence in their skills, and experiences with the district's curriculum reform (this last set of questions was used in an earlier RAND evaluation of district curriculum reforms). Specific items changed slightly as implementation of PPIP evolved but generally addressed the same broad set of topics. The primary purpose of the survey was to gather quantifiable information on principals' practices and opinions about various aspects of PPIP. For each wave of survey administration, principals were informed that their responses would be confidential and that any reporting would be done in the aggregate. Principals did not receive any financial incentives for participating in the survey.

The mode of administration was selected based on input from the district and varied over time. In spring 2008, we administered paper-and-pencil surveys to all PPS principals during a regularly scheduled principals' meeting. All principals who attended the meeting provided responses to the survey (n = 61 of 65, a 94-percent response rate) but we were unable to obtain information that would allow us to identify principals, so these first-year data cannot be linked to principals' schools or to subsequent surveys. These data were used exclusively to provide formative feedback to the district and are not included in the analyses presented in this report.

In spring 2009, we administered the survey via the web. The survey link was emailed to principals, and periodic reminders were sent to nonrespondents. We received responses from 38 out of the 65 principals who were recruited,[1] for a response rate of 58 percent. The respondents were reasonably well balanced across schools representing different grade-level configurations but included a disproportionate percentage of novice principals (40 percent of the survey respondents were novices, compared with 29 percent novices in the district as a whole).[2] The survey was similar to one that was administered during the first year of the evaluation, described above.

In the third year of the evaluation, spring 2010, we again used web-based administration. We received responses from 48 out of the 67 principals who were recruited, for a response rate of 72 percent. The sample included reasonable representation across different types of schools; it included more than 60 percent of K–5, K–8, and special schools (those serving special populations of students) and 100 percent of middle

---

[1]   This study focused on principals who participated in the formal evaluation process. PPS reported that there were 68 principals in the district in 2008–2009, but three of these were not formally evaluated because they were in the position of acting principal. Our analyses focused on the remaining 65.

[2]   Novice principals are those who are in their first two years as principal or who have more than two years of experience and are in their first year of service to PPS. Principals who are new to the position remain a novice for two years. Experienced principals in their first year of service to PPS remain a novice for one year.

schools. However, only 38 percent of the district's high schools were represented in the sample. The sample also provided good representation across novice and experienced principals, with response rates exceeding 70 percent in each group. The survey was similar to one that was administered during the first and second years of the evaluation but also included new questions about the Teaching and Learning Team (TLT) visits.

The final round of survey administration occurred in spring 2011. Discussions with the district suggested that in-person administration might improve response rates, so we administered a paper survey to PPS principals during a regularly scheduled all-principals meeting. Principals were asked to write the name of their school on the first page of the survey, tear that sheet off and return it to the research team, and then complete the survey; nearly all principals did so. We matched the first pages with the surveys (both were numbered) and were thus able to identify principals and link these survey responses with those from previous years. The sample included reasonable representation across different types of schools; it included more than 80 percent of K–5 schools, 100 percent of K–8, 9–12, 6–12 schools, 60 percent of special schools, and more than 75 percent of middle schools. The sample also provided good representation across novice and experienced principals, with response rates of 80 percent in each group.

For survey questions that were identical in years 2, 3, and 4, we created a data file that linked individual principals' responses and examined changes in these responses over time among the set of principals who had responses in each of the three years. We created a similar linked file for the set of principals with responses in years 3 and 4. Sample sizes for linked responses from years 2 through 4 ranged from 11 to 23, depending on the survey item, and sample sizes for linked responses from years 3 and 4 ranged from 12 to 32, depending on the item. Findings from the linked data need to be interpreted with extra caution because of the small sample sizes and the unrepresentative nature of this group, but they are useful for understanding the extent to which changes in survey results over time reflect actual changes in principals' opinions or practices, as opposed to changes in the cohort of principals who responded to the survey or differences across years in the characteristics of principals or the schools they served. Most of the findings in the report that refer to changes over time use these linked data files.

Coach Surveys

We surveyed coaches during years 1, 3, and 4 of the PPIP evaluation; we describe method of administration, response rates, and survey content in this section. Coaches are expert teachers who spend a majority of their time providing support and feedback to other teachers. Most coaches specialize in a subject area—typically, either math or English language arts (ELA). In Pittsburgh, some coaches are assigned to a single school or grade level, whereas others work in more than one school or grade level. We did not survey coaches in year 2 because of budget constraints. The survey administered in year 1 was developed primarily for another district evaluation but included a set of questions that asked respondents to rate their principals on several dimensions of leadership. It was used exclusively for formative purposes and is not included in this report. In years 3 and 4, we developed a coach survey that included several questions that aligned with the principal survey. It included questions about in-school data use and professional development, TLT visits, coaches' opinions of their principals' leadership skills, and perceived changes in their principals' behavior and time allocation since the beginning of PPIP.

In each of the three years, the survey was administered via the web to all district coaches. As with the principal survey, coaches received the survey link via email, and periodic reminders were sent to nonrespondents. Coaches were informed that their survey responses would be confidential and that any reporting would be done in the aggregate. In year 1, we received surveys from 111 of 129 coaches, for a response rate of 86 percent. As with principals, no financial incentives were offered to coaches for participating in the survey.

In year 3, we received responses from 74 of the 112 coaches who were recruited, for a response rate of 66 percent. The sample included good representation across different types of schools; it included more than 75 percent of K–5, K–8, and 6–8 coaches, and more than 60 percent of high school, special school, and Accelerated Learning Academy (ALA) coaches.[3]

In the final year, we received responses from 60 of the 77 coaches who were recruited, for a response rate of 78 percent. We are unable to provide grade level–specific response rates because, in 2010–2011, many coaches worked across grade levels. However, the sample included coaches from all grade levels and school configurations, including ALAs, with the exception of special schools, from which there were no coach respondents.

Teacher Survey

We did not conduct a teacher survey as part of this evaluation, but, during year 4 (2010–2011), we administered a teacher survey as part of the Intensive Partnership Sites evaluation, which was funded by the Bill and Melinda Gates Foundation to examine reforms in four sites across the United States, including the Empowering Effective Teachers (EET) initiative in PPS. We use one set of teacher survey items from that evaluation in this report; this set of items examines teachers' perceptions about the quality of their school administrators' leadership and is relevant to understanding the PPIP reforms.

---

[3] ALAs are schools that are designed to help students who are performing below grade level improve to grade-level performance. ALAs have a longer school day and a longer school year than other schools and additional professional development for instructional staff. The curriculum is grounded in the America's Choice School Design Model (see Pearson, undated).

The teacher survey sample included between ten and 25 teachers in each PPS school (the number sampled varied by school size). The stratified random sampling procedure took into account subject area and experience level. We administered the survey via the web, sending the link to teachers by email, along with periodic email reminders to nonrespondents. We surveyed 842 teachers, and 657 submitted responses to the surveys, for a response rate of 78 percent. As with the principal and coach surveys, all teachers were informed that their survey responses would be confidential and that any reporting would be done in the aggregate. Teachers received a payment of $25 for completing the survey.

Interviews with Building-Level Staff

We conducted interviews with principals and other school staff in each year of the evaluation. The primary purpose of conducting interviews was to complement the surveys, specifically by eliciting responses with richer detail and greater depth. Each interview was conducted by a member of the research team who used a structured protocol to guide the questioning. Probe questions were also used as needed to follow up. In all cases, the researcher took detailed notes, which were later coded for specific themes. All participants were informed that their interview responses would be confidential and that any reporting would be done in the aggregate. Participants were also informed that no responses or quotations would be reported in a way that would allow them to be identified. We used a different approach to interview data collection each year as a means of providing both depth and breadth. Specifically, two rounds of interviews involved a small sample of school visits during which we interviewed a variety of school staff, whereas the other two rounds relied on telephone interviews that enabled us to reach larger numbers of participants and schools, as discussed in this section.

Year 1 (2007–2008): School Case-Study Visits

In spring 2008, we randomly selected eight schools for in-person visits. Schools were selected based on their grade configuration so that we achieved a representative sample. Building-level interviews were conducted at four K–5 schools, two K–8 schools, one middle school, and one high school. We interviewed all principals (eight), all reading and math curriculum coaches who were available on the day of our visit (15), and a sample of teachers (21) individually. Teachers were selected based on the content and grade level they taught (e.g., teachers were selected who taught mathematics or reading or English across a mix of grade levels). All school staff invited to participate did so. Principal and coach interviews each lasted between one and two hours, whereas the teacher interviews lasted approximately 30 minutes.

Year 2 (2008–2009): Principal Interviews

In spring 2009, we contacted each principal by email and phone to request her or his participation in an individual telephone interview. Forty-seven out of the 65 principals who were recruited participated in the interview, for a response rate of 72 percent. Principals were informed that their interview responses would be confidential and that any reporting would be done in the aggregate. As with the principal survey, we obtained a reasonable degree of balance across school types and principal experience levels. Most interviews lasted 30–45 minutes, but a few were significantly longer. The interviews addressed principals' reactions to the components of PPIP, particularly the rubric and achievement bonus, their professional development and interactions with their assistant superintendents and TLTs, and their leadership practices.

Year 3 (2009–2010): School Case-Study Visits

In fall 2009, we recruited ten schools for case-study visits and were able to secure permission to visit from eight of these schools. There were not the same schools we visited in year 1. Case-study schools were selected to ensure variability along several dimensions relevant to PPIP: grade-level configuration, level of principal experience (novice or experienced), total 2008–2009 PPIP payout (high, medium, or low), and 2009–2010 evaluation (rubric or a DPG project). Special schools were excluded from the sample. Case studies consisted of a telephone interview with the principal in fall 2009 and an in-person visit to the school in spring 2010. During the in-person visit, we conducted interviews with the principal; two coaches, if applicable; and three teachers. In schools that had two coaches, we interviewed both coaches; in schools that had more than two coaches, we sampled coaches who were second and third alphabetically by last name. Teachers were sampled by grade configuration using a process designed to ensure variability and representativeness (e.g., in K–5 buildings, we interviewed the first-grade teacher whose last name appeared first in the alphabet, the third-grade teacher whose last name appeared last in the alphabet, and the fifth-grade teacher whose last name appeared first in the alphabet).

We conducted fall interviews with seven of the eight principals sampled (one principal did not respond to our request) and spring interviews with all eight principals. All teachers and coaches contacted with a request to participate consented. Most interviews lasted 30–45 minutes. The interviews addressed participants' reactions to PPIP and other reforms, their school improvement initiatives, the environment in their schools, professional development and other supports provided to them, and other relevant topics.

Year 4 (2010–2011): Interviews with Principal/Coach Pairs

In fall 2010, we recruited 13 principal/coach pairs for individual telephone interviews, and were able to secure permission to speak with nine principal/coach pairs. We interviewed two additional principals but were unable to contact the coaches at those schools. Interviewee pairs were selected to ensure variability along several dimensions relevant to PPIP: grade-level configuration, level of principal experience (novice or experienced), total 2009–2010 PPIP payout (high, medium, or low), and 2010–2011 evaluation (rubric or a DPG project). If the school had more than one coach, we selected the coach whose last name was first in the alphabet, and we ensured that the sample included mathematics coaches and literacy specialists (ELA coaches). Special schools were excluded from the sample. Interviews consisted of separate telephone interviews with the principal and the coach in spring 2011, and most interviews lasted 45–60 minutes. The interviews addressed participants' reactions to PPIP and other reforms, their school improvement initiatives, the environment in their schools, professional development and other supports provided to them, and other relevant topics. The primary reason for interviewing principal/coach pairs was to assess the extent to which principals and coaches in the same schools shared similar views on leadership practices and on the school environment.

Interviews and Email Communications with District-Level Staff and External Consultants

Throughout the evaluation, we interviewed or conducted focus groups with district-level staff and consultants to provide additional background information on the implementation of PPIP and on broader changes in district policy or practice. In December 2007 (year 1), we conducted a focus group with the assistant superintendents.[4] In years 2 and 3, we conducted individual interviews with several district staff, including the deputy superintendent, the chief academic officer, and all of the assistant superintendents throughout the 2008–2009 and 2009–2010 school years. The content of the interviews varied depending on the district official's role, but each interview was designed to provide information relevant to understanding the district's TOA and the implementation of various program elements. In year 4, we conducted individual interviews with all district-level staff who had been in the assistant superintendent role during the 2010–2011 school year. These interviews took place at various times during summer 2011. The content of the interviews was similar to that in years 2 and 3, and the interviews were also designed to provide information relevant to understanding the district's TOA and the implementation of various program elements. We also drew on email exchanges with district staff throughout the four years of the evaluation to document implementation issues and changes to the program elements.

Reviews of Documentation

Throughout the four years of the evaluation, we gathered extensive documentation from the district, including minutes from steering committee meetings, TLT protocols and tools, updates to the rubric and bonus payout qualifications, and information about principal professional development.

---

[4] In 2007–2008, the assistant superintendents were called *executive directors*. The position title changed at the beginning of the 2008–2009 school year.

Principals' Scores on the Administrators' Performance Standard Rubric

PPS provided RAND with a deidentified file containing scores on each of the rubric components, along with indicators for school grade configuration, principal experience level (novice or experienced), whether the school was an ALA, and salary increment amount.

Student Data

We obtained student scores on the Pennsylvania System of School Assessment (PSSA) tests and the 4Sight benchmark assessments for all students in the district who took these tests.[5] We also obtained student demographic information, including gender, race (African American or non–African American), and free or reduced-price lunch (FRL) status, as well as student course-taking information. All this information was retrieved from the district's Real Time Information (RTI) student data system. RTI also provided each student's home address, which was geocoded so that it could be linked with census tract–level information on poverty and adult educational attainment. RTI contains most student information back as far as the 1999–2000 school year. However, the achievement growth measures require testing in consecutive grades, which did not occur until 2005–2006. All of these data were made available by the district through the 2010–2011 school year. Other data, such as the counts of graduating seniors who took the SAT exam, were obtained in aggregate form from the district.

Analytic Approach

As described in the previous section, we drew on multiple sources of data, each of which was intended to complement the others. In this section, we briefly describe our analytic methods for each major source of data used in this report. Additional details are provided in the relevant chapters where appropriate.

Principal, Coach, and Teacher Survey Data

For each survey item, we calculated descriptive statistics, including frequencies, means, and standard deviations. With the exception of the teacher survey data, we did not apply weights to these frequencies because our sample sizes were small and we lacked sufficient information about the characteristics of responders and nonresponders to enable the generation of weights. Therefore, it is important that readers recognize that the results cannot be generalized to the district as a whole. Teacher survey responses were weighted to adjust for nonresponse, and the high response rate on that survey (78 percent) allows for generalizability to the district's full teacher population.

---

[5] The PSSA is a statewide standardized test that is administered in grades 3–8 and in grade 11. Student scores on the PSSA are ranked according to four achievement levels: below basic, basic, proficient, and advanced. In Pennsylvania, AYP is assessed according to the PSSA. See Pennsylvania Department of Education, undated.

In addition, we also created two linked survey data sets for the principal data. One data set included all principal survey items that were identical in years 2 (2008–2009), 3 (2009–2010), and 4 (2010–2011), and the second included all principal survey items that were identical in years 3 and 4. We used the linked principal data to examine changes in responses over time. We examined the magnitude of the differences and conducted tests of significance (paired t-tests) for the change in scores on each item (using a significance level of 0.05) in the years 2–4 linked data and for the linked data in years 3 and 4. Because these analyses are fairly exploratory and we are not attempting to generalize from a sample to a broader population, we did not adjust the significance levels to address multiple comparisons. Therefore findings of statistically significant differences should be interpreted cautiously. Although we looked at differences in responses across categories of principals, including grade configuration of the school and whether the principal was novice or experienced, we do not report on these differences because of small sample sizes. The body of the report presents survey results that are most relevant to our key findings, but all of the descriptive survey results from the year 4 survey and the two linked data sets are presented in Appendix D (published separately, available for download). Frequencies from previous years of survey data were provided to the district via internal memos as part of RAND's role as formative evaluator.

Factor Analysis

We conducted a series of exploratory factor analyses using the year 3 and year 4 principal survey data and coach survey data to identify sets of items that could be clustered together into scales. For each set of items, we first excluded items for which more than 30 percent of the responses were missing or not applicable, and then conducted a principal components analysis with orthogonal (varimax) rotation. Decisions about the number of factors to retain in each case were made based on a combination of empirical considerations (e.g., scree plots) and the need for scales that would be substantively meaningful and informative. We then generated scales by calculating the average item-level response across the items assigned to a scale for each respondent. Table A.1 in Appendix A (published separately, available for download) lists the principal survey scales, the items assigned to the scales, and the estimate of internal consistency reliability (coefficient alpha) for each scale, and Table A.2 summarizes the coach survey scales.

Interviews with Building-Level Staff

We used a consistent analytic approach for the interviews with building-level staff conducted in each year of the evaluation. Interviews were analyzed using a framework developed by the research team, which allowed for documentation of responses by respondent group. The coding scheme was derived from the TOA, but coders also noted other issues that emerged. After coding, coders extracted key themes relevant to each code and placed them in a template, allowing coders to look across schools and respondent types. We examined the consistency of coding by having two research team members independently analyze sets of case interview data from two schools and compare their data templates. When the data in an individual cell of the template were not consistent across the two coders, we returned to the original interviews to ensure that consistent definitions were being applied. After this check for consistency of the coding scheme, the remaining interviews were coded by one researcher. All of the interview responses were open-ended and were coded in two ways. First, statements were coded for common themes that directly addressed the research questions of interest. Second, in some cases, the interviews generated additional themes or topics that were relevant to the report; this often occurred in response to probing questions. In these cases, new themes and topics were identified and responses were coded according to these themes or topics. Following the initial analyses of the interview data, we reread each section of the framework, reviewed the original interview data, and sought to validate findings through triangulation with other sources of data.

District Interviews and Document Review
The document review and interviews with district staff served multiple purposes, including informing our understanding of the program elements and their implementation. We used these data to inform and update our understanding of PPIP elements and to help us interpret and contextualize the data we gathered from principals and other school staff.

Rubric, Achievement, and Bonus Data
We calculated some basic descriptive statistics to examine performance on rubric, achievement, and bonus measures for the district as a whole and in relationship to student characteristics. In year 3, the district implemented a bonus premium for principals in "high-need schools," which meant that the bonus was no longer determined only by student achievement. Therefore, we separately analyzed the relationship of achievement with student characteristics and the relationship of the bonus with student characteristics. We also conducted some correlational and exploratory factor analyses to understand the relationships among these measures, as well as the relationships among standards and components on the rubric, though readers should keep in mind that the sample sizes are small and these results need to be interpreted with caution. The details of these analyses are provided in Chapters Six and Seven.

Method for Linking and Jointly Analyzing Rubric and Achievement Data
The rubric scores were considered confidential personnel information and so could not be passed to the evaluator in any way that was linked with information that identified the individual principal or his or her school. Therefore, we devised a set of spreadsheets that contained the school-level achievement and demographic data and embedded formulas that jointly analyzed the rubric and achievement data when PPS cut and pasted

the rubric data into the reserved areas. These formulas calculated cross-tabs, correlations, and regressions and stored the estimates in separate worksheets that could be sent separately to the research team without revealing the rubric information on individual schools. In this way, we could examine relationships among rubric information, achievement information, and school demographic information in a manner consistent with the need to preserve confidentiality of personnel data.

Limitations

It is important to keep in mind the limitations of the data sources and methods used in this evaluation. In particular, the group of principals who chose to participate in the surveys and interviews is not necessarily representative of the population of PPS principals. Moreover, responses are likely to vary across school types (e.g., elementary versus secondary schools) and across principal experience levels, but we avoid breaking the data down by these categories because of the small numbers of principals in each category. The quantitative analyses of the rubric are based on a fairly small sample of principals who were evaluated using the rubric, so caution is warranted when making inferences based on the findings of these analyses. An additional limitation is a lack of independent measures of some of the intermediate and ultimate outcomes, including measures of principal skill and knowledge and independent, non–high-stakes measures of student achievement. Perhaps most importantly, and as noted earlier, because the reform was implemented district-wide, in the context of numerous other significant changes, causal inferences about the effects of PPIP on principal practices or student outcomes are not warranted.

CHAPTER THREE

District Context and Pittsburgh Principal Incentive Program Theory of Action

The evaluation included an effort to elucidate the district's implicit TOA for PPIP. This TOA describes the outcomes the district was trying to achieve and the mechanisms through which it expected the program to achieve those outcomes. Following the CIPP model (described in Chapter Two), the TOA provides a framework for understanding the context in which PPIP was implemented, the inputs (the program elements that constitute the intervention), the process of how the program elements were implemented, and ultimately, the product, or the success of the program according to its goals.

The CIPP model emphasizes that an understanding of the context in which an intervention takes place is necessary for a high-quality evaluation. PPIP was one of several district-wide reform initiatives, and a full evaluation of PPIP requires an understanding of its alignment with these other initiatives. For instance, it is important to understand whether the goals of PPIP are aligned with those of other district programs, what effect other programs could have on the implementation and functioning of PPIP (particularly in terms of time demands on participants), and where PPIP fits in the context of the district's strategic plan. Importantly, the district context of multiple ongoing reforms, all of which have similar overlapping goals, makes it impossible to attribute any findings directly to PPIP. Therefore, it is critical that the findings in this report be interpreted in the context of multiple reforms in which PPIP was implemented. In this chapter, we provide some background for understanding PPIP implementation by briefly discussing related reform initiatives under way in the district, present an overview of the TOA, provide a brief summary of major implementation changes during the four years of PPIP, and finally describe the use of the TOA in this report.

District Context and Related Reforms

PPIP is one local manifestation of the national focus on improving school leadership as a means of promoting effective teaching and student achievement. PPIP was implemented, and continues to function, in a reform-oriented district in which it is one of many ambitious initiatives in place.

In recent decades, PPS, along with the city of Pittsburgh, has been suffering population decline, such that the district's capacity in 2005 was for 50,000 students but only about 30,000 were enrolled (see Young, 2007). Enrollment decline, in conjunction with poor performance, nearly led to state takeover of the district in 2005. In response to this threat, the superintendent was tasked with streamlining district operations and improving student performance. As a result, the superintendent launched a strategic plan for district-wide reform, Excellence for All (EFA), which was introduced in May 2006. Broadly, the goals of the EFA program were to improve district operations, improve student achievement, and reduce racial achievement gaps by implementing a comprehensive series of reform initiatives. The initiatves were implementing a new, managed curriculum; providing instructional coaches; providing a safe learning environment for students; setting goals for minority student participation in college-preparatory and advanced coursework; and focusing on recruiting and training principals and holding them accountable for student achievement.[1] One important component of the EFA plan was an effort to "right-size" the district by reducing the operating deficit and consolidating district operations. In February 2006, the district closed more than 20 schools as part of its right-sizing plan.[2]

It is important to understand that the PPIP TOA we present and track in this report operates as one piece of the district's larger EFA reform strategy. EFA brought a new focus on principals as instructional leaders, and PULSE, one component of which was PPIP, was implemented in the 2007–2008 school year to meet the EFA goal of focusing on recruiting, training, and supporting principals.

In the 2006–2007 school year, after the implementation of EFA and the right-sizing process, the district implemented ALAs in schools that had been struggling to make achievement gains. The eight ALAs use the America's Choice instructional model and offer a longer school day and year.[3] Additionally, ALA teachers and principals receive targeted professional development in the America's Choice model; as a result, ALA principals have both extra resources and extra demands, which may influence how they respond to the capacity-building interventions and incentives of PPIP.

Also in the 2006–2007 school year, the district initiated a focus on assessing and improving the high school experience, created the High School Reform Task Force, and charged members with creating a plan that would decrease the drop-out rate, sup-

---

[1] For a complete description and evaluation of the EFA plan, see Tharp-Taylor, Nelson, Dembosky, and Gill, 2007, and Tharp-Taylor, Nelson, Hamilton, and Yuan, 2009. Also, see PPS, undated (c).

[2] The right-sizing plan took school performance into account by drawing on a RAND study of school achievement trajectories (Gill, Engberg, and Booker, 2005). See PPS, 2006.

[3] Because of school closings and reconfigurations, the district had seven ALAs at the time of this report. See PPS, undated (a).

port students as they transitioned to high school, and ensure that seniors graduated with a postsecondary plan. Implementation of the resulting plan, *Excel.9–12: The Plan for High School Excellence*, began that same year and spurred implementation of several programs designed to complement Excel.9–12 (PPS, undated [b]). Among those programs were 9th Grade Nation, a program designed to support students as they transition to high school and that included team-building and leadership experiences during the ninth-grade year, as well as a civics curriculum. The district also provided new secondary learning options, in the form of magnet schools.[4] In addition, the district continued to reevaluate its enrollment, facilities, and operations and to merge, close, or reconfigure schools in accordance with the goals of EFA and the right-sizing plan.

In 2007, the district announced the Pittsburgh Promise scholarship program,[5] which, in alignment with the goals of EFA and Excel.9–12, broadly aimed to support postsecondary planning and attendance by providing eligible students with "last-dollar"[6] grants to cover the cost of postsecondary education. Specifically, the goals of the Promise were to enable more PPS students to pursue postsecondary education, to increase enrollment in city schools, and to serve as a measure of how well the district helps students prepare for postsecondary education. This was a significant change in the landscape of incentives schools face in raising student achievement because Promise eligibility criteria provided schools and individual students with clear targets for academic performance.[7]

The most recent addition to the slate of reform initiatives was a district-wide program to improve student achievement and student preparation for postsecondary goals by focusing on improving teaching effectiveness. In 2008–2009, in response to teacher feedback, the district developed the Research-Based, Inclusive System of Evaluation (RISE), a new system for observing and evaluating teacher practice and for guiding teacher professional growth. In 2009, based in part on the RISE work, the district received substantial funding from the Bill and Melinda Gates Foundation to implement the EET program, the goal of which is to fully prepare more students for postsec-

---

[4] These four new magnet schools—the Pittsburgh High School for the Creative and Performing Arts (Pittsburgh CAPA), University Prep 6–12 at Milliones (Pittsburgh Milliones), the Barack Obama Academy of International Studies (Pittsburgh Obama 6–12; formerly Pittsburgh Frick/Pittsburgh IB), and the Pittsburgh Science and Technology Academy—are open as of the writing of this report and offer students a variety of advanced coursework and project-based learning options. Although these schools are open to all students, each school has additional eligibility requirements (see PPS, 2010).

[5] The Promise was established by the district in partnership with the University of Pittsburgh Medical Center (UPMC), which made the initial financial commitment, and with the City of Pittsburgh. To be eligible for a Promise award, students must maintain a 90-percent attendance record and a 2.5 grade point average, be a graduate of a PPS school, and be a student in the district and a resident of Pittsburgh continuously since at least the ninth grade. Promise scholarship funds must be applied to a Pennsylvania state-funded school, community college, or private school. Two- and four-year programs and trade schools are eligible.

[6] Last-dollar funding is applied to education expenses after state and federal grant funds.

[7] See Gonzalez et al., 2011, for an evaluation of the Pittsburgh Promise scholarship program.

ondary education, such that 80 percent of PPS students will complete a college degree or postsecondary training certification.

The EET goals were highly consistent with the reform initiatives that predated it (see Appendix B, published separately). EET had three priorities: "(1) increase the number of highly effective teachers; (2) increase the exposure of high-need students to highly effective teachers; and (3) ensure [that] all teachers work in learning environments that support their ability to be highly effective" (PPS, 2009, p. 2.)[8] Further, many aspects of the EET work, and of RISE in particular, were consistent with PPIP and can inform the context in which PPIP developed. For example, the RISE process provided differentiated support to teachers based on their years of teaching experience, just as PPIP provided differentiated support to principals based on their level of experience. Additionally, from its inception, the rubric that was used to evaluate principals encouraged principals to spend more time in classrooms observing and coaching teachers; the RISE process not only provided the framework for this task but also prompted changes to the rubric and to the supports and professional development provided to principals as part of PPIP. Increasing alignment between principal and teacher evaluation rubrics has the potential to strengthen implementation of both programs by reinforcing common goals and a shared language around them. Targeted, in-school professional development for teachers is also a central component of EET and of RISE, which complements the PPIP objective of principals serving as instructional leaders who can design and deliver more-targeted professional development for their teachers. The EET program also includes mechanisms and incentives, such as new career paths for teachers that come with additional compensation, to attract high-performing teachers to high-need schools, just as some PPIP incentives were designed to attract highly effective principals to high-need schools. At the time of this report (spring 2012), the district was in the third year of implementing the EET reforms and was facing a severe budget shortfall. Despite the funding challenges, district and PFT leadership remained committed to implementing the EET reforms.

Taken together, the designs of these reform initiatives appear to be well-aligned and to contain mechanisms that support the district's broad strategic goals of attracting, developing, and retaining excellent principals and teachers; improving student achievement; improving college readiness and attendance; and improving educational equity, thus providing a context that both supports PPIP implementation and com-

---

[8]   Additionally, the EET work includes reforms to many district offices, systems, and processes. For example, in addition to RISE for evaluating teacher classroom practice and supporting teacher growth, the district is working to develop a comprehensive measure of teacher effectiveness, which will include a value-added measure of teacher performance and the rubric-based teacher observation measure. In partnership with the Pittsburgh Federation of Teachers (PFT), the district is in the process of restructuring its human resources structure and systems and its teacher recruitment and hiring practices, creating new career paths for teachers, designing and implementing new compensation structures for teachers, and creating new or revamping existing data systems to support these efforts. In July 2010, the district and the PFT ratified a new collective bargaining agreement that codified many of these reform efforts.

plicates interpretation of the effects of PPIP. The timeline of implementation of these reforms is summarized in Figure 3.1. This discussion provides some understanding of the context in which PPIP currently operates, as well as a sense of the ways in which the context of overall district reform has influenced the development and implementation of PPIP.

Theory of Action Overview

Our TOA is designed to identify the ultimate and intermediate goals of PPIP and to specify the means by which the design of PPIP could meet these goals, thereby providing a framework for both external evaluation and internal program improvement. Conversations with district staff, along with reviews of PPIP documentation, helped us identify the outcomes that the district intends PPIP to attain, as well as the strategies that it has developed in the service of reaching these goals. We also vetted the TOA with key district staff at intervals during the evaluation.

The TOA is pictured in Figure 3.2. The ultimate goal of PPIP is to improve student achievement throughout the district. The italicized phrases in this narrative summary of the TOA correspond to the levels of the visual representation, starting at the top with district-wide interventions and tracing their intended impacts to the student

Figure 3.1
Timeline of Reform Activities in Pittsburgh Public Schools

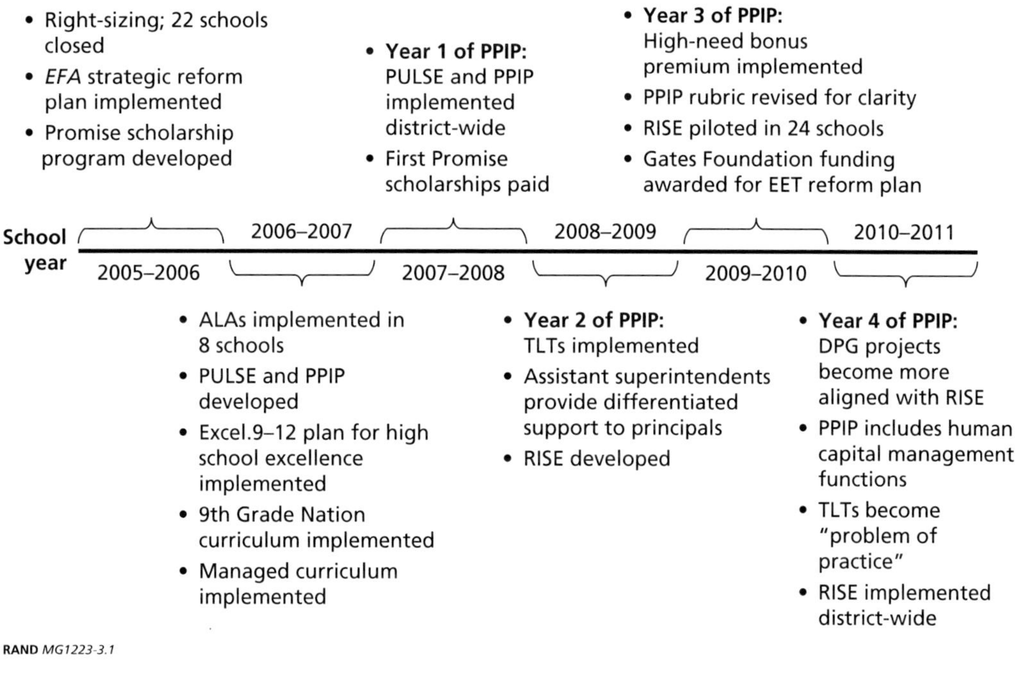

- Right-sizing; 22 schools closed
- *EFA* strategic reform plan implemented
- Promise scholarship program developed

- **Year 1 of PPIP:** PULSE and PPIP implemented district-wide
- First Promise scholarships paid

- **Year 3 of PPIP:** High-need bonus premium implemented
- PPIP rubric revised for clarity
- RISE piloted in 24 schools
- Gates Foundation funding awarded for EET reform plan

School year: 2005–2006   2006–2007   2007–2008   2008–2009   2009–2010   2010–2011

- ALAs implemented in 8 schools
- PULSE and PPIP developed
- Excel.9–12 plan for high school excellence implemented
- 9th Grade Nation curriculum implemented
- Managed curriculum implemented

- **Year 2 of PPIP:** TLTs implemented
- Assistant superintendents provide differentiated support to principals
- RISE developed

- **Year 4 of PPIP:** DPG projects become more aligned with RISE
- PPIP includes human capital management functions
- TLTs become "problem of practice"
- RISE implemented district-wide

RAND *MG1223-3.1*

Figure 3.2
Pittsburgh Principal Incentive Program Theory of Action

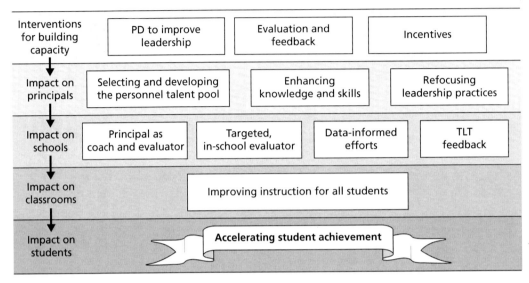

RAND *MG1223-3.2*

level. PPIP includes a set of *capacity-building interventions* that are intended to improve student achievement through a causal pathway that starts with the improvement of the quality of instructional leadership provided by principals. This *impact on principals* is hypothesized to take place through three possible mechanisms: selecting and developing the pool of principals (e.g., by encouraging high-quality leaders to apply for positions), enhancing the knowledge and skills of principals, and refocusing principals' leadership practices to emphasize activities that are likely to improve student achievement. Changes in principal practices could come as a result of principals working longer or harder, or they could reflect a reallocation of principal time and effort toward some activities at the expense of others. All of these effects on principals are intended to lead to *impact on schools*—e.g., increased focus of all school staff on using data for instructional decision making. These school-level changes are then expected to produce *impact on classrooms* by improving the quality of instruction, which should lead to the ultimate *impact on students*: improved achievement. The five levels of the TOA illustrate this hypothesized pathway. Although the TOA represents the components of PPIP in discrete boxes, it is important to recognize that, in practice, many of the elements have impacts on multiple levels. In particular, several capacity-building interventions are means of evaluation and feedback, in addition to being forms of professional development.

We provide more detail on each level, as well as trace the evolution of the district-level capacity-building interventions (i.e., professional development to improve leadership, evaluation and feedback, and incentives) in the rest of this section. Of course, it is important to recognize the influence of district context on PPIP, but, for simplicity, we did not include it in the depiction of the TOA.

Interventions for Building Capacity

The "Interventions for building capacity" level of the TOA describes PPIP elements that are designed to increase the capacity of principals to serve as instructional leaders and includes three broad categories: (1) professional development to improve leadership, (2) evaluation and feedback, and (3) incentives. In this section, we briefly describe each of these elements and summarize any major changes that occurred during the four years of PPIP implementation.

Professional Development to Improve Leadership

PPIP has an extensive professional development component that is designed to build principal capacity by providing principals at all levels of experience with the support necessary to serve as effective leaders of their schools. Professional-development offerings range from a training program for new principals, to sessions focused on instructional leadership, to one-on-one coaching with their supervisors. However, it is important to note that, as the district has implemented multiple reforms with similar goals (e.g., RISE), these professional-development opportunities have evolved to support those programs as well, making it difficult to attribute specific professional-development mechanisms to PPIP. The professional-development opportunities available to principals are summarized in Table 3.1. Additionally, the district has provided professional-development sessions to, at first, inform principals about PPIP, and, in

Table 3.1
Professional Development Opportunities Available to Principals

Professional-Development Program	Description of Content[a]	Changes During PPIP Implementation	Eligible Principals[b]
PELA	Intensive, yearlong program for principals in training; can include experiences, such as serving as "acting" principal under the guidance of an experienced principal		PELA fellows
PAIA	Intensive support for novice principals over one or two years; includes building management and instruction, as well as intensive training on the rubric and evaluation process		Novice principals

Table 3.1—Continued

Professional-Development Program	Description of Content[a]	Changes During PPIP Implementation	Eligible Principals[b]
Leadership Academy	Large-group professional-development sessions, generally conducted at one of the professional learning centers in the district; presented throughout the school year and for one week before start of the school year		All principals
Focus on Results	Grade level–specific professional development with a focus on specific instructional improvement strategies and building culture		K–5 principals in years 1–3; K–5 and 5 high schools in year 4
America's Choice	Targeted professional development offered to ALA building principals		ALA principals
TLT visits	Periodic school visits by a group of curriculum content, instructional, and data experts to provide feedback to principals	Called "problem of practice" in some schools in year 4	All principals
Assistant superintendent coaching	One-on-one coaching sessions with assistant superintendent to discuss student data, rubric evidence, and principal reflections on practice	In year 3, assistant superintendents differentiated support by school achievement level; this practice continued through year 4[c]	All principals
In-school professional development	Targeted sessions for teachers, generally designed by principals, curriculum coaches, or the instructional leadership team; also includes learning walks, conducted by the principal and ITL		All principals
DPG projects	Yearlong projects on a topic chosen by the principal; completed in two out of every three years	In year 4, all DPG projects were aligned with RISE, the new teacher observation measure	Experienced principals

NOTE: PAIA = Pittsburgh Administrator Induction Academy. ITL = instructional teacher leader.

[a] Descriptions of professional-development program content provided here are examples; the list is not exhaustive.

[b] Eligibility as of year 4 (2010–2011).

[c] Starting in the 2011–2012 school year, assistant superintendents adjusted the method for providing differentiated support based on school performance, such that struggling schools were paired with high-performing schools as another source of support.

later years, provide updates on changes to PPIP. For example, during year 2 of PPIP implementation, new principals received training specific to PULSE and PPIP, and experienced principals had the opportunity to attend PPIP-specific training during the summer Leadership Week.

Evaluation and Feedback

PPIP evaluation and feedback components are designed to build principal capacity by setting clear, measurable goals for improving principal leadership and by providing consistent, structured feedback to principals to guide principals' efforts to improve their practices.

Mechanisms for Evaluation

Prior to PPIP, assistant superintendents were responsible for working with principals to ensure that district curricula were being implemented with fidelity and that principals were engaging in effective leadership of their schools.[9] With the implementation of PPIP in the 2007–2008 school year, the standards-based rubric became the primary mechanism by which principals were evaluated. Assistant superintendents use the rubric to evaluate principal practice, provide feedback, and guide professional-development and support opportunities. Principals use the rubric to guide their efforts to attain and demonstrate proficiency in practical areas within a defined structure; scores on the rubric are linked to additional compensation opportunities.

The original rubric (see Appendix C, published separately, for a description of rubric standards and changes), which was in use in the years 1 and 2 of PPIP, includes seven standards, each with three or four components,[10] on which principals were rated by their assistant superintendents across four levels of performance: rudimentary, emerging, proficient, and accomplished. Evaluation of principals across these levels of performance is intended to be evidence-based, which requires the evaluator to draw on facts, rather than opinion or hearsay, during the evaluation. The district defines *evidence* as a factual reporting of events, which may include teacher, principal, and student actions or behaviors, as well as instructional artifacts.

The rubric underwent some revisions at the start of year 3 of PPIP. These revisions were based on feedback from principals during the first two years of implementation and were made in an effort to simplify and clarify the rubric standards and performance levels and clarify the standards for evidence. More-substantial revisions to the

---

[9] At the start of PPIP, the district had five assistant superintendents, each of whom worked with principals in a specific type of school (e.g., K–5 schools, ALAs). That number dropped to four in year 4 of PPIP as a result of school closings and reconfigurations. Assistant superintendents are former principals, and, in the first two years of PPIP implementation, a consultant hired by the district trained assistant superintendents in how to coach and evaluate principals.

[10] The rubric was developed in 2006–2007 by a committee composed of central office staff, principals, and consultants from the Educational Testing Service (ETS), working in consultation with the RAND research team. Six of the seven original rubric standards were based on standards for principal leadership described by the Interstate School Leaders Licensure Consortium (ISLLC) (see Council of Chief State School Officers, 2008), each of which had four components. The district added a seventh standard, with three components, based on the body of research in principal leadership available at the time (e.g., Halverson, 2005; Marzano, Waters, and McNulty, 2005).

rubric were implemented at the start of year 4 of PPIP, in response to principal feedback and the EET reforms described earlier. These involved eliminating standards 6 and 7 and revising the first two standards to focus on human capital management and teacher evaluation and coaching, an adjustment that brought the rubric into greater alignment with RISE and other concurrent teacher effectiveness reforms implemented as part of EET.

The evaluation process and degree of support were designed to differ across levels of principal experience. Novice principals, who are new to administration or new to the district, are formally evaluated, using the rubric, once per semester for either two or four semesters. A novice principal's formal evaluation focuses on rubric standards 1, 2, and 3, but novices are expected to self-evaluate on all standards and components and to identify areas for growth.

Experienced principals are grouped into three cohorts; each cohort is evaluated on all rubric standards once every three years. In his or her evaluation year, an experienced principal is expected to collect evidence, participate in a midyear and year-end self-assessment, in collaboration with his or her supervisor. During the intervening two years, when the experienced principal is not engaged in formal evaluation, he or she participates in DPG projects under the supervision of his or her assistant superintendent. DPG projects, which are also linked to additional compensation, allow principals to select a rubric component on which they wish to improve and design a program of growth based on that component. In year 4 of PPIP, when the district was implementing RISE, its new measure of teacher practice, the district asked principals to focus their DPG projects on topics related to improving student and teacher growth, which resulted in a natural alignment of the DPG process with RISE implementation.

In year 4 of PPIP, the new rubric standards 1 and 2, which, as described earlier, focused on human capital management and evaluation and coaching of teachers, became the evaluation focus for novice and experienced principals. That is, principals were required to collect evidence only for standards 1 and 2; there was no longer a requirement that principals collect evidence relevant to the other standards unless a problem was noted by the assistant superintendent. Functionally, principals were rated as proficient on standards 3 to 5 unless there was evidence to the contrary; if a principal wanted to be rated accomplished, he or she had to provide evidence to support that rating.

Principals who exhibit rudimentary performance according to the rubric may be placed on an improvement plan at the discretion of the assistant superintendent. Principals who are placed on an improvement plan receive an official notification from the district and are encouraged to access district resources, such as additional support or research articles, for improving performance. Principals on improvement plans are not evaluated on the rubric, but their progress is monitored by their assistant superintendents.

Mechanisms for Feedback: Assistant Superintendent Coaching

There are two major mechanisms for building principal capacity by providing feedback within PPIP: feedback provided by assistant superintendents and feedback provided as part of TLT school visits. Assistant superintendents are responsible for principal evaluation, for providing principals with support and feedback that will help improve their performance, and for ensuring that principals have access to appropriate professional development. Feedback provided by assistant superintendents is designed to support capacity building in the areas emphasized by the rubric. The balance between providing feedback as professional development to support growth on the rubric standards and conducting an evaluation that leads to a financial reward for principals' work can be a delicate one for assistant superintendents.

In year 1 of PPIP, assistant superintendents were expected to provide principals with feedback during one-on-one coaching sessions, which generally took place in the context of visits to the schools. Assistant superintendent coaching in year 2 became a more formalized process and was provided primarily within the context of the TLT visit. TLTs were instituted in response to challenges faced by the assistant superintendents during building visits in year 1. Through principal feedback, district staff learned that the assistant superintendent visits were perceived as evaluative and did not provide principals with an adequate amount of support for curriculum study and student data analysis. In response to this feedback, the district supplemented the assistant superintendent visits with TLT visits. In year 2, assistant superintendents provided differing levels of support to principals, depending on the achievement level of the school, with lower-achieving schools receiving more support.

Mechanisms for Feedback: Teaching and Learning Teams

TLTs consist of curriculum content experts, a special education expert, staff from the district's Research, Assessment and Accountability office, and experts in grade level–specific programs or subjects, as appropriate.[11] TLT visits, as they occurred in years 2 and 3 of PPIP, followed a consistent format: beginning with analysis of relevant student achievement data (e.g., Dynamic Indicators of Basic Early Literacy Skills [DIBELS] or 4Sight scores, interim classroom assessments, grades, discipline or attendance data) and discussion of the next steps determined during the previous visit, along with progress made, after which the TLT conducts classroom observations using a feedback form developed for the purpose.[12] While the TLT is conducting classroom observations, the principal and the assistant superintendent meet one-on-one for a coaching session. At

---

[11] For instance, at the K–8 level, the TLT includes a curriculum content expert in science, along with Reading First and pre-K experts.

[12] 4Sight is a diagnostic test designed to predict students' performance on the PSSA and is administered in grades 9 and 10. 4Sight topics and test questions were specifically developed to correlate with the PSSA and serve as a performance benchmark. 4Sight was included to provide measurements in grades 9 and 10 because the PSSA is not administered at all grade levels.

the end of the visit, the TLT, principal, and assistant superintendent reconvene to share feedback from the classroom visits and discuss next steps. In addition, assistant superintendents continue to visit schools and meet with principals one-on-one.

In year 4, the TLT process was revised based on feedback from principals and as a result of new support needs that arose as the district implemented elements of the EET reforms, including RISE, its new teacher evaluation system. The year 4 TLTs focused on a school's "problem of practice," an instructional problem identified by the principal. Although evidence was still collected through classroom observation, TLT guidelines were revised to clarify procedures for collecting evidence and providing feedback and to adjust the structure of the visits to be less disruptive to the schools.

Throughout PPIP, assistant superintendents were also expected to be available to principals via email and telephone on an as-needed basis. TLT visits and differentiated assistant superintendent support continued in years 3 and 4 of PPIP.

Incentives

The most public component of PPIP is the set of financial incentives offered to principals, which are designed to serve not only as financial rewards but also as a means of offering recognition to effective principals. The monetary reward has two components, both of which were implemented in the 2007–2008 school year and which remained in place, albeit with some changes, through year 4 of PPIP: a salary increment of up to $2,000 and an achievement bonus of up to $10,000. The salary increment, which is retained in base pay, is based on the principal's performance on the rubric or on a DPG project, as well as on the school's AYP status and the principal's tenure. The achievement bonus is calculated annually and not retained in the principal's base pay; it is calculated primarily using a set of student achievement measures.

Salary Increment
Eligibility for the top salary increment amounts, $1,500 for novice principals and $2,000 for experienced principals, was linked to scores on the rubric, as well as achieving AYP as required by No Child Left Behind (NCLB). Principals participating in DPG projects were also eligible to receive the performance increment, and, in year 2 of PPIP, eligibility for the full increment for principals on DPG projects became linked to achieving AYP as well. PPIP salary increments are summarized in Table 3.2.

Achievement Bonus
In consultation with RAND research team members, an Achievement Bonus Subcommittee, which consisted of district central office staff and principals, developed the achievement measure on which the yearly principal bonus of up to $10,000 is based. The bonus provides an incentive for principals to adopt behavior and practices

Table 3.2
Pittsburgh Principal Incentive Program Salary Increment Amounts

Award Tier	Novice		Experienced		DPG		
						Requirements	
	Amount ($)	Requirements	Amount ($)	Requirements	Amount ($)	Year 1	Years 2–4
1	1,500	Majority of performance at proficient or accomplished levels; no rudimentary performance; AYP met	2,000	Proficient or accomplished performance on all standards; no rudimentary performance; AYP met	2,000	Satisfactory completion of the project	Satisfactory completion of the project; AYP met
2	1,000	Majority of performance at proficient or accomplished levels; no rudimentary performance; AYP not met	1,500	Majority of performance at proficient or accomplished levels; no rudimentary performance; AYP not met	1,500	Not applicable	Satisfactory completion of the project; AYP not met
3	500	Emerging, proficient, or accomplished performance; no rudimentary performance; AYP not met	1,000	Emerging, proficient, or accomplished performance; AYP not met; no rudimentary performance			

NOTE: Majority is defined as 12 or more components, with each component receiving one of four ratings.

that align with increasing student achievement, reducing the socioeconomic and racial achievement gaps, and with district performance goals under the EFA reform agenda and AYP as required by the NCLB legislation, without penalizing principals who work in challenging schools. When it was implemented in year 1 of PPIP, the achievement bonus measure consisted of three components: the School Performance Index 2 (SPI-2) regular; the SPI-2 third-grade reading emphasis; and high school measures. In year 3 of PPIP, a "high-need premium" was added to the achievement bonus. In year 4, the high school version of the SPI-2 regular and one of the high school measures were replaced with new measures. Each of these measures is described briefly in this section.

SPI-2 Regular

The SPI-2 regular was designed to measure student achievement growth in mathematics and reading. The SPI-2 regular measures average percentage growth in students' scaled standardized test scores from the previous year. For example, in the 2007–2008 school year (year 1 of PPIP), the SPI-2 regular compared students' scaled standardized scores on the 2007–2008 tests with their scores on the 2006–2007 tests. A student who has a scaled score of 800 in 2006–2007 and a scaled score of 880 in 2007–2008 would have exhibited 10 percent growth. The SPI-2 regular was primarily based on scaled scores in mathematics and reading from the PSSA test in grades 3–8 and grade 11. The original design also used the reading component of the 4Sight test in grades 9 and 10 and the math 4Sight in grade 10.

By measuring percentage growth over time, the SPI-2 provides incentives for principals to focus on previously low-achieving students. To continue the previous example, 80 points of growth shown by a student who had a scaled score of 1,600 in the 2006–2007 year would translate to only 5 percent growth in 2007–2008, whereas the student with the scaled score of 800 and 80 points of growth shows 10 percent of achievement growth. Principals are eligible for the full bonus amount if at least 10 percent growth in both mathematics and reading is achieved school-wide. The decision to use scaled scores reflects principals' desire to receive credit for growth that does not necessarily move the student from one achievement level to the next (e.g., from basic to proficient). Any principal whose students had an average growth of 10 percent would receive the maximum amount allocated for the achievement growth portion of his or her bonus, with proportionately lower amounts awarded to principals with lower growth. The properties of the measure were examined using data from the 2004–2005 and 2005–2006 school year to ensure that it would not unfairly reward principals of schools with students of particular characteristics. Existing variation in score growth within and among schools was also examined to determine that there was likely to be meaningful variation in bonuses among schools but not so much as to place unsustainable financial burden on the district.

In year 4, the district discontinued the use of the 4Sight tests in high school, which meant that a new achievement growth measure needed to be developed for high school students. The district decided that this would be a good opportunity to begin to align the RISE measures with the PPIP measures. Therefore, the steering committee met with RAND and Mathematica (the value-added measure [VAM] contractor) and decided to create a new measure based on the average of the full set of RISE school-level VAMs based on the PSSA, PSAT (Preliminary SAT), and locally developed curriculum-based assessments covering most academic high school subjects. The new measure is converted to have the same mean and standard deviation as the high school SPI-2 regular during years 2 and 3, which allows the bonus to be awarded using the same 0- to 10-percent growth scale. Of note, the RISE measure rewards absolute rather than percentage growth, thereby removing one of the two methods by which the bonus provided an incentive to reduce achievement gaps.

SPI-2 Third-Grade Reading Emphasis

District-level concern with improving reading achievement at the third-grade level prompted the inclusion of a SPI-2 regular component to emphasize and reward increases in third-grade reading achievement. This measure is also included because schools' efforts to promote achievement in grades K–3 would not be rewarded. This component is calculated by comparing the scaled PSSA reading score of each third-grader to the scaled PSSA reading scores of third-grade students with similar characteristics during the previous two years (the comparison score). The comparison score is calculated using multiple student characteristics, such as gender, race/ethnicity, socioeconomic status, and neighborhood characteristics.

Given the difficulty of matching each current student with an identical student from a prior year, the comparison score was predicted from a regression equation in which the above-listed student characteristics were explanatory variables. Performance scores are calculated by subtracting the comparison score (the predicted scaled score) from the actual scaled score, dividing by the comparison score, and multiplying by 100. Percentage differences are averaged within each school. Principals of schools with achievement gains of 10 percent or greater would be eligible for the full bonus amount. Principals who demonstrate achievement gains of 0 to 10 percent are awarded prorated bonuses.

High School Measures

The high school–specific measures align with the district's goals for reducing the socioeconomic and racial achievement gaps and improving graduation and college readiness rates and are designed to provide an incentive for principals to direct resources to improvement in these areas. These measures are also included to counteract any unintended incentive contained in the achievement growth measure that rewards principals at schools where low-achieving students drop out. Students must be enrolled in a school for at least three months to be counted in the measure. We discuss the specifics of each high school measure below:

- Number of African American students taking college-level courses: Expected yearly district-wide growth is apportioned to each high school based on the proportion of PPS African American students in 11th and 12th grades who attend each high school. Schools with larger populations of African American students thus have higher numeric targets for the required increase in African American students taking college-level courses.
- Increase in the number of students taking college-level examinations: District-level expected yearly growth is apportioned to high schools based on the proportion of PPS students in 11th and 12th grades who attend each high school; schools with larger populations of students have higher numeric targets for the required increase in students taking college-level examinations.
- Increase in the number of college-level examinations with satisfactory scores: District-level expected yearly growth is apportioned to high schools based on the proportion of PPS students in 11th and 12th grades who attend each high school; schools with larger populations of students have higher numeric targets for the required increase in students achieving satisfactory scores on college-level examinations.
- Increase in the percentage of graduating seniors who take the SAT exam: District-level expected yearly growth is apportioned to high schools based on the proportion of PPS graduating seniors who attend each high school; schools with larger populations of students have higher numeric targets for the required increase in graduating seniors who take the SAT exam. The required percentage of graduating seniors who take the SAT exam is capped at 90 percent; schools that attain the 90-percent rate automatically qualify for the bonus regardless of the rate the previous year.
- Increase in the percentage of students who earn 6.5 credits or more: This measure tracks the number of students who make adequate progress to graduation during the current year. Students who earn 6.5 credits in a year are deemed to be on track and making adequate process toward graduation. Students who earn fewer than 6.5 credits in the current year may be categorized as making adequate progress toward graduation as long as the student has accumulated sufficient credits in previous years to be on track to graduate during his or her senior year. A principal was awarded the maximum amount if the percentage of on-track students was 95 percent or had increased by at least 6 percentage points and was awarded one-half that amount for a three-point gain. In year 4, this measure was replaced with the EET VAM based on high school core course completion. Similar to what was done for the new high school achievement growth measure, this new on-track measure was converted to the scale of the old measure to maintain continuity.

High-Need School Premium

The formula used to calculate principals' performance on the achievement bonus measures and the dollar amounts attached to each type of measure was revised during year 2 of PPIP and implemented at the start of year 3. These changes were partly the result of changes in the grade configurations of some schools. However, the most important change was the addition of a high-need school premium. One of PPIP's initial goals was to attract high-performing principals to schools populated by students with the biggest challenges. The high-need premium is based on several measures that represent those challenges, and, starting in year 3, all schools were ranked on the following four measures: percentage of students eligible for FRL, percentage of students with (nongifted) individualized education programs (IEPs), percentage of adults who are high school drop-outs in students' residential neighborhoods, and average income in students' residential neighborhood relative to the poverty line. The average of the ranks for each school was then calculated, and schools were again ranked based on this average rank. The top one-fourth of schools was classified as high need.

The top four schools in this ranking were given a bonus premium of 100 percent. That is, for any level of performance on the bonus measures, their principals would be given bonuses twice as large as those awarded to principals in non–high-need schools. However, high-need school principals' bonuses were still capped at $10,000. Whereas a non–high-need school principal would need achievement growth of 10 percent (or a comparable value on the other measures) to obtain a $10,000 bonus, this group of the four highest-need schools could obtain a $10,000 bonus with 5 percent achievement growth. The next group of four would be able to obtain the full bonus with 6 percent achievement growth, the next with 7 percent, and the remaining high-need schools with 8 percent achievement growth. In this fashion, the district gave higher rewards on a sliding scale to principals in high-need schools for similar achievement growth. This element of the achievement bonus remained in place in year 4, although the rankings were revised based on year 3 school characteristics. The achievement bonus measures are summarized in Table 3.3.

Determination of Bonus Award Amounts

The total bonus of $10,000 is allocated differently across the measures described earlier by school grade level. The steering committee endeavored to assign dollar amounts to these achievement goals that reflected the relative importance of the goal. Bonus amounts are summarized by component and by grade level in Table 3.4.

The $2,000 high school measures award is distributed among its specific goals as described in Table 3.5.

Although the principals of ALAs were operating under a pay-for-performance system that was separate from PPIP and that included opportunities to earn a $10,000 bonus based on measures of student achievement growth and adoption of best practice

Table 3.3
Summary of Achievement Bonus Measures

Measure	K–5	K–8	6–8	6–12	9–12
SPI-2 regular	Based on PSSA scores in math and reading	Based on PSSA scores in math and reading	Based on PSSA scores in math and reading	Based on PSSA scores in math and reading (grades 6–8) Based on PSSA and 4Sight scores in math and reading (grades 9–12, years 1–3) or RISE school-level VAMs (grades 9–12, year 4)	Based on PSSA and 4Sight scores in math and reading (years 1–3) or RISE school-level VAMs (year 4)
SPI-2 third-grade reading emphasis	Based on PSSA scores in reading (grade 3 only)	Based on PSSA scores in reading (grade 3 only)	N/A	N/A	N/A
High school measures	N/A	N/A	N/A	Based on district goals for reducing the socioeconomic and racial achievement gaps and on measure of students on track to graduate	Based on district goals for reducing the socioeconomic and racial achievement gaps and on measure of students on track to graduate

NOTE: N/A = not applicable. Beginning in year 3, all schools were ranked based on four student characteristics: percentage receiving FRL, percentage special needs, poverty level of home neighborhoods, and adult educational attainment of home neighborhoods. These rankings in each category were averaged, and schools were ranked again on this average. The top quarter of schools were designated high need and had reduced requirements for bonus attainment.

standards, ALA principals were also eligible for the additional compensation under PPIP.

Throughout PPIP, principals of special schools, which serve populations of challenged or gifted students, have been eligible for the $2,000 salary increment but were not eligible for the $10,000 bonus during the first year of PPIP, because of equity concerns. Even though special-needs students are evaluated according to an alternate assessment, the steering committee decided that the bonus measures did not provide a fair assessment of academic growth. Consequently, the district applied for and was granted permission to change the scope of the project to exclude principals of special schools from eligibility for the $10,000 bonus for the first year of PPIP. These principals were, however, paid $3,000 in the first year as a participation bonus to attempt to develop a plan that would allow them to receive the student achievement bonus even-

Table 3.4
Bonus Achievement Measure Maximums ($)

Level	SPI-2 Regular	SPI-2 Third-Grade Reading Emphasis	High School Measures	Total
K–5	6,000	4,000	N/A	10,000
K–8	8,000	2,000	N/A	10,000
6–8	10,000	N/A	N/A	10,000
6–12	9,000	N/A	1,000	10,000
9–12	8,000	N/A	2,000	10,000

NOTE: Some schools that have 6–12 grade configurations did not open as such but are adding a grade level each year. These schools are included in the 6–12 category.

Table 3.5
High School Measure Award Amounts ($)

High School Measure	School Type	
	9–12	6–12
Increase in the number of African American students taking college-level courses	200	100
Increase in the number of students taking college-level exams	200	100
Increase in the number of college-level examinations with satisfactory scores	200	100
Increase in the percentage of graduating seniors who take the SAT exam	400	200
Increase in the percentage of students who earn 6.5 credits or more (year 1-3) or core-course completion VAM (year 4)	1,000	500
Total	2,000	1,000

NOTE: Some schools that have 6–12 grade configurations did not open as such but are adding a grade level each year; 6–12 schools that have not yet added grades 11 and 12 are not eligible for the on-track bonus.

tually. Although the U.S. Department of Education initially required the district to include principals of special schools in the bonus measures, the district was unable to do so in a way that was fair and equitable.

Impact on Principals

A critical question regarding the district's approach is whether each of the capacity-building interventions discussed in the previous section improves the quality of school leadership in the district. The TOA posits that these interventions are likely to operate through at least one of three possible mechanisms: (1) the reshaping of the principal talent pool (e.g., by attracting more reform-minded leaders into principal positions in the district); (2) the enhancement of principals' knowledge and skills, particularly in the area of instructional leadership; and (3) changes in principals' practices. Moreover, principals could change their practices in a variety of ways, including working harder (i.e., devoting more time to their work), working more efficiently, and reallocating time from activities that are less central to the district's goals in order to devote more time and effort to the desired activities. Our conversations with district staff suggest that many of the elements of PPIP, including the rubric and the professional development, were intended primarily to promote skill development and reallocation of time and effort.

Impact on Schools

The PPIP TOA hypothesizes that the capacity-building interventions discussed in the previous section—professional development to improve leadership, evaluation and feedback, and incentives—will, by changing principal behavior, have a positive impact at the school level. PPIP is expected to have a positive effect at the school level in four ways: (1) by increasing use of data to guide instruction; (2) improving targeted, in-school professional development opportunities for teachers; (3) allowing principals to provide specific, constructive feedback to teachers as a result of the TLTs; and (4) encouraging principals to focus on instruction as coaches and evaluators of teachers.

Impact on Classrooms and Students

The TOA suggests that PPIP's impact on schools will then produce positive effects on classrooms—in the form of improved instruction—and on students, ultimately improving student achievement. By developing stronger instructional leaders, the district intends to enable principals to work collaboratively with their school staffs to improve the quality of instruction through various mechanisms, including improving the fidelity of curriculum implementation and providing teachers with the tools and support they need to use assessment data effectively. These efforts are then intended to raise student achievement. Achievement is conceptualized broadly to include not only test scores but also measures of attainment, such as course-taking and graduation rates.

This final evaluation report is structured around the TOA. We focus first on the top three levels—the implementation of the interventions and their impacts on principals and schools—and then we discuss impact on classrooms and on student achievement. Readers should keep in mind that PPIP was implemented in the context of other district reform efforts, and therefore it is difficult to isolate the effects of PPIP on principal leadership and student performance.

CHAPTER FOUR

Capacity-Building Interventions

In this chapter, we discuss principals' responses to the capacity-building interventions that PPS adopted to support principals as part of PPIP. We examine the three categories of interventions depicted in the TOA: professional development, evaluation and feedback, and incentives.

Professional Development

As discussed in Chapter Three, PPS provided a variety of professional-development opportunities to principals. These included formal, workshop-style professional development, such as the summer Leadership Academies, as well as less formal professional learning experiences, such as the interactions that principals had with their assistant superintendents. Because these supports are likely to be critical to the success of PPIP, our surveys and interviews included several questions to gauge principals' opinions about the quality and utility of the professional development. We discuss the results in this section.

Principals viewed participation in their DPG projects and learning walks with their instructional teams as large contributors to their professional growth. On the 2011 principal survey, principals were asked to rate how much each of several professional development experiences in the 2010–2011 school year contributed to their professional growth using a four-point scale (1 = not at all, 2 = a small amount, 3 = a moderate amount, and 4 = a large amount). As shown in Figure 4.1, several forms of professional development were rated as moderate or large contributors to principals' professional growth by more than two-thirds of principals who responded to the items. Principals' learning walks with their own instructional leadership teams, the Leadership Academies, and professional development outside the district were among the most–highly rated forms of professional development. Notably, more than half of responding principals rated their participation in their own DPG projects as large contributors to their growth, suggesting that this activity was particularly valuable for principals who engaged in it. The fact that principals were expected to focus their DPGs on improving student and teacher growth, topics that naturally align with the RISE teacher evaluation tool, in year 4

Figure 4.1
Principals' Reports Regarding the Extent to Which Professional Development Contributed to Their Professional Growth, Year 4

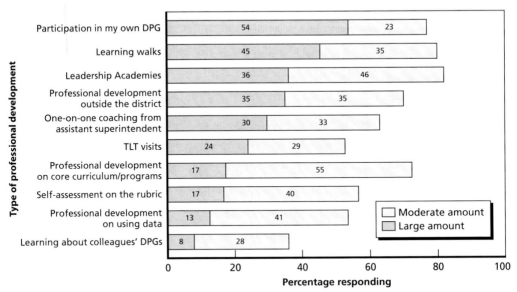

NOTE: The survey item read, "How much did each of the following experiences from this school year (including summer) contribute to your professional growth as a principal? (If the item is not applicable, choose N/A)." Percentages exclude principals who indicated that the item was not applicable. Sample sizes ranged from 26 to 61. Items addressing DPGs and self-assessment on the rubric have smaller sample sizes than other items because only a subset of principals participated in these activities. Responses were given on a scale of 1 = not at all, 2 = a small amount, 3 = a moderate amount, 4 = a large amount, 5 = not applicable. Responses are sorted in descending order by percentage reporting a large amount.
RAND MG1223-4.1

could provide one explanation for the perceived value of this activity because principals reported RISE being a primary focus of their work in general that year. In the year 4 interviews, nine of 11 principals reported satisfaction with the supports provided them to meet PPIP goals. However, most of the supports they mentioned were not specific to PPIP; training related to RISE and Focus on Results were the supports most frequently cited as valuable. Newer principals were particularly satisfied with the support they received and praised the "strong induction program," referring to the PELA program.

Principals' ratings of the value of Leadership Academies and learning walks declined between year 3 and year 4. Because the same question was asked on the principal surveys in years 2, 3, and 4 of PPIP, we were able to examine how principals' opinions about the utility of various forms of professional development changed as PPIP matured (see Tables D.2 and D.3 in Appendix D, published separately, for summaries of the three-year and two-year linked results, respectively). Although none of the changes across the full three-year period was statistically significant, in part because of the small number of principals who completed the survey all three years, a few statistically significant changes were observed between years 3 and 4. Principals were less likely in year 4 than in year 3 to describe Leadership Academy professional development and learning walks with their own instructional team as making large contributions to their professional growth. It is possible that this decline is partly a result of the fact that these principals had participated in these forms of professional development for at least two years and, in some cases, for longer and consequently did not believe they had as much to gain from these experiences in year 4. In addition, the interviews indicated that professional development focused on RISE was overshadowing other forms of professional development in year 4, and several principals suggested that some professional development they received was not as strongly focused on PPIP as it should have been. Some principals made a direct comparison between PPIP and RISE-related training and found the PPIP training less valuable.

DPG projects were reportedly helpful to the principals conducting them but had less impact as a tool for sharing practices and lessons among principals across the district. The district intended for DPGs to serve as learning opportunities for the principals who carry out the projects and for their colleagues, with whom principals were expected to share their DPG work. Figure 4.1 shows that, although 54 percent of principals who completed a DPG in year 4 indicated that it had a large effect on their professional growth, only 8 percent described learning about other principals' DPGs as having a large impact on their growth. In addition, the year 3 survey asked principals to indicate how much impact their DPG had on several aspects of their jobs, ranging from no impact to substantial impact. The findings provide further indication that DPGs were valued by principals as an individual exercise related to improving their schools or their practice rather than as a means of sharing best practices among peers. For example, 50 percent of principals reported a substantial impact on the development of specific new strategies of practice used in their schools, whereas only 25 percent reported a substantial impact on "strategies, lessons or practices from my DPG being used by *other* principals in the district" (see Table D.29 in Appendix D). Given that most DPGs addressed the common topic of RISE in year 4, there was an opportunity for collaborative learning and exchange of information, but the survey responses suggest that, for the most part, principals did not perceive that this learning occurred. Nonetheless, the positive reactions of principals to their work on their own DPGs suggest that this was a valued activity.

Most principals reported a positive impact of Leadership Academy participation on their instructional leadership. We asked principals to indicate whether participation in Leadership Academy professional development helped them develop their leadership capacity in several areas. As shown in Figure 4.2, nearly 90 percent of principals agreed or strongly agreed that the Leadership Academy professional development helped them in the area of monitoring teachers' instruction, and more than three-quarters agreed or strongly agreed that this form of professional development helped them provide useful feedback on teachers' instruction. In only four areas did a majority of principals agree or strongly agree that the Leadership Academy training was valuable: provide effective

Figure 4.2
Principals' Perceptions of Value of Leadership Academy Professional Development for Helping Develop Their Leadership Skills, Year 4

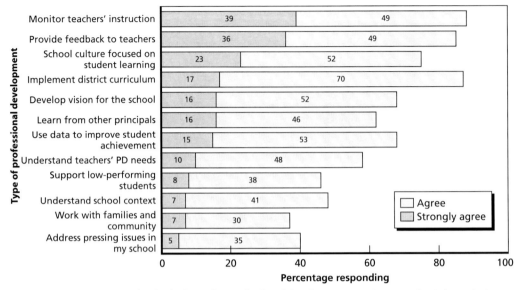

NOTE: The survey item read, "Think about the professional development you have received through the Leadership Academies. To what extent do you agree or disagree with these statements? Overall, the professional development I have received through the Leadership Academies has helped me to. . . ." Sample sizes ranged from 60 to 61; N may vary across items because of missing responses. Responses were given on a scale of 1 = strongly disagree, 2 = disagree, 3 = agree, and 4 = strongly agree. Responses are sorted in descending order by percentage responding that they strongly agree.
RAND MG1223-4.2

supports to low-performing students; work effectively with families and community members; understand the broader political, social, economic, legal, and cultural context in which my school operates; and address the most-pressing issues in my school. These findings are consistent with the district's decision to emphasize instructional leadership in its professional development for principals and suggest that principals value Leadership Academy professional development as a source of support for helping them develop into effective instructional leaders.

An examination of the three-year and two-year linked data (Appendix D, Tables D.5 and D.6, respectively) show that principals' opinions of the utility of Leadership Academy professional development declined between years 3 and 4 in several areas, such as using data to improve student achievement and learning from other principals. Principals' opinions of Leadership Academy professional development were generally more positive in year 3 than in year 2 or in year 4. The qualitative data do not suggest an obvious explanation for this change, although, as noted earlier, other forms of professional development that focused on RISE were provided in year 4, and the salience of this RISE-focused professional development might have led to a reduction in the perceived relative utility of the Leadership Academies. One principal commented about the Leadership Academy, "For the role of instructional leader, I would say [that I am] not very satisfied. It is fine for managerial roles. RISE on the other hand is all about instruction." In addition, we found that, in year 4, novice principals assigned lower ratings to the Leadership Academy professional development than did their more experienced counterparts, although, with only a small number of novices (nine to 11, depending on the item), these differences need to be interpreted cautiously.

Evaluation and Feedback

Although the evaluation and feedback provided to principals by their assistant superintendents can be viewed as a form of professional development, we treat it separately in the TOA because of its critical role in facilitating principals' success on the PPIP measures. The first set of results in this section documents principals' perceptions of the value of their interactions with assistant superintendents. This information is useful for understanding the nature and intensity of feedback and support principals are receiving.

Nearly two-thirds of principals reported that one-on-one coaching from their assistant superintendents made a moderate or large contribution to their professional growth. Assistant superintendents are expected to serve as both evaluators and mentors to help principals improve their practice as coaches and evaluators of teachers and as instructional leaders. Thirty percent of principals surveyed responded that "one-on-one coaching from [their] assistant superintendent" had contributed a large amount to their professional growth as a principal during year 4, with an additional 33 percent responding that such coaching contributed a "moderate" amount (see Figure 4.1). Compared with other PPIP supports, one-on-one coaching from the assistant superintendent was the fifth-most valued of ten possible supports, ranking below DPGs and Leadership Academy professional development but above TLT visits and self-assessment on the rubric, similar to its relative ranking in year 3. Comparing the case study data from years 3 and 4, some principals reported receiving less support from their assistant superintendents in year 4. In year 3, all of the principals in the school case studies acknowledged that support and coaching from their assistant superintendent was helpful, though four of the eight noted that their assistant superintendent support was primarily helpful for navigating district mandates and policies rather than for principals' professional growth. In the year 4 interviews, eight of the 11 principals interviewed mentioned assistant superintendent coaching when asked broadly about what supports the district provided to help them meet PPIP goals. Of those eight, three said that their assistant superintendents provided little or no support and two said that their assistant superintendents were helpful with policy, managerial, and district communication issues but not with instructional leadership. New principals tended to express more satisfaction with how their assistant superintendents supported their instructional leadership, and two specifically mentioned the value of assistant superintendent involvement with their DPGs.

Principals reported high-quality support for communication from their assistant superintendents. In the survey, principals were asked to rate the quality of support they received from their assistant superintendents on a four-point scale (1 = poor, 2 = fair, 3 = good, and 4 = excellent). Table 4.1 indicates the percentage of principals who provided a rating of "good" or "excellent" for each item, and full results are provided in Appendix D, Table D.7. Areas for which assistant superintendents were most likely to be rated as excellent pertained to communication: Thirty-nine percent of principals rated assistant superintendent support as excellent in the area of communicating in a clear and timely way about district policy, and 37 percent provided this rating for communicating principals' concerns or suggestions to other central office staff. Smaller percentages of principals gave ratings of excellent in areas related to evaluating

Table 4.1
Percentage of Principals Rating Assistant Superintendent Support as Good or Excellent, Year 4

Response	Good	Excellent
Communicating in a clear and timely way about district policy	31	39
Communicating your concerns or suggestions to other central office staff	33	37
Acquiring needed resources for your school	30	30
Providing fair and accurate feedback on your performance	31	28
Coaching you on providing feedback that helps your teachers to improve their instruction	27	27
Helping you identify your leadership strengths and weaknesses	31	25
Helping you support teachers on improvement plans	31	23
Helping you improve your rubric performance	25	20
Coaching you on how to evaluate your teachers	37	18
Providing support for curriculum implementation in your building	38	16
Helping you select professional development that meets your own needs	35	15
Helping you design professional development for your staff	30	10
Supporting your work on your DPG project	56	22

NOTE: The survey item read, "Please rate the quality of the support you have received from your assistant superintendent this year (including one-on-one meetings during TLT visits) in each of the following areas." Responses are sorted in descending order by percentage responding that support was excellent. Percentages may not sum to 100 because of rounding. Sample sizes ranged from 60 to 61. Responses were given on a scale of 1 = strongly disagree, 2 = disagree, 3 = agree, 4 = strongly agree, and 5 = not applicable. Principals who responded "not applicable" to the question about DPG projects are omitted from the calculations for that item. Sample size for this item is 18.

teachers, supporting curriculum implementation, selecting or designing professional development, and supporting work on the DPG, but, in a majority of areas, as shown in Appendix D, Table D.7, more than half of principals rated assistant superintendent support as either good or excellent in most areas.

Analysis of the linked data on this survey item showed that principals' ratings of assistant superintendent support on the communication items remained constant or improved over time, whereas ratings on items related to principal leadership development and curriculum implementation and supporting or evaluating teachers declined from year 3 to year 4. This is somewhat surprising in light of the growing emphasis the district is placing, via RISE, on principals' roles as coaches and evaluators of teachers.

When we asked assistant superintendents what topics they focused on when giving feedback to principals, they reported working with principals on leadership skills, on strategies to utilize other building instructional leaders (such as coaches and ITLs), and on coaching and observing teachers. In addition, assistant superintendents said they focused on supporting principals who have teachers on improvement plans and on helping principals identify "what proficient looks like" on the rubric. Some assistant superintendents noted that they spent less time with principals they were "not worried about" and instead focused on principals who needed more support. It is possible that, in some cases, the assistant superintendents underestimated the extent to which principals wanted additional support on instructional leadership activities, leading to the perception among some principals that support could be improved in these areas.

Most principals viewed the TLTs as having the right mix of expertise, but fewer than half said that teachers viewed the TLT visits as constructive and nonevaluative. The TLTs provide another mechanism through which the district supports principals in their work as school leaders. As discussed in Chapter Three, TLTs, which are now called "problems of practice" in some schools, are designed to provide nonevaluative, team-based support to principals. TLTs consist of a variety of district-level staff, such as curriculum content specialists and data specialists. The primary mechanism of TLT support is a structured school visit, which includes classroom observations and culminates with the TLT members providing feedback to the principal and, generally, the school leadership team. Approximately two-thirds of year 4 principal survey respondents agreed or strongly agreed that the TLTs brought the right mix of expertise to support the school's needs, and a similar percentage reported that the TLTs gathered fair and actionable data about instruction during their visits. Several principals commented that the new "problem of practice" approach was helpful in targeting the mix of expertise to the specific needs of the school being visited. Overall, however, TLT visits ranked fairly low among the most-valued supports for PPIP. As Figure 4.1 earlier in this chapter shows, just over half of principals rated TLT visits as having contributed a large or even moderate amount to their growth, placing them ninth of the ten supports rated.

Although two-thirds of the principals agreed or strongly agreed that the TLT process was collaborative and nonjudgmental, fewer agreed or strongly agreed that teachers in their buildings viewed the TLT feedback as constructive and nonevaluative (see Figure 4.3). This pattern was even more pronounced in coaches' views of the TLT visits. Although 58 percent of coaches thought TLT visits were collaborative and nonjudgmental, 86 percent of coaches agreed with the statement "Most of the teaching staff feels they are being evaluated when the TLT visits." Chapter Five presents data on the perceived impacts of the TLT process on school practices.

Figure 4.3
Principals' Opinions of Teaching and Learning Team Visits, Year 4

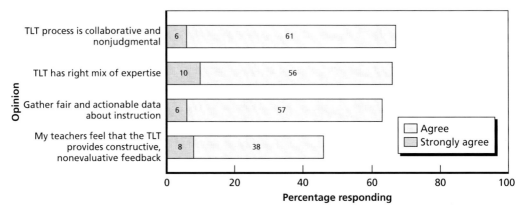

NOTE: The survey item read, "Please indicate your level of agreement with the following questions about Teaching and Learning Team (TLT) visits to your school during the current school year (2010–2011)." Sample sizes ranged from 50 to 51. Responses were given on a scale of 1= strongly disagree, 2 = disagree, 3 = agree, and 4 = strongly agree. Responses are sorted in descending order by percentage agreeing (i.e., the sum of "strongly agree" and "agree" responses).
RAND MG1223-4.3

Incentives

PPIP provided three broad sets of incentives to principals: an annual salary increment that was determined primarily by performance on the rubric, an annual bonus based on measures of student outcomes at the school level, and a bonus for working in high-need schools. Principals' responses to these incentives are likely to have a large impact on the ultimate success of the program. In this section, we examine principals' responses to each of these incentives.

Principals viewed the rubric as helpful and realistic but were concerned about fairness and consistency of ratings across assistant superintendents. As shown in Table 4.2, a large majority of principals in year 4 reported that the rubric-based evaluation process helped them think about their leadership strengths and weaknesses, which suggests that the rubric has value as a professional development tool. Majorities also reported that they had a clear understanding of the targets they needed to reach and that the targets were realistic. Moreover, hardly any principals agreed that the evaluation process had exerted a negative effect on their relationships with their assistant superintendents, which suggests that the supportive role that assistant superintendents were expected to play was not hindered by their roles as evaluators. Another positive finding is that only 16 percent of principals agreed or strongly agreed with the statement "It will be relatively difficult for me to earn a salary increase this year because conditions in my school prevent me from engaging in the practices specified by the rubric." This is encouraging because it suggests that most principals are taking responsibility for their own practices and not blaming students or school conditions for poor performance on the rubric.

As we discussed in Chapter Three, the district made some changes to the rubric and the evaluation process, and the survey and interview data suggest that the changes were well received. In year 4, 38 percent of principal survey respondents agreed or strongly agreed with the statement "The Administrators' Performance Standard Rubric contains so many standards and components that I can't possibly address all of them," compared with 48 percent in year 3 (see Appendix D, Table D.26). Principal interview participants in year 4 reported that the rubric that was being implemented that year was more focused than it had been in the past and that it was well-aligned with the work principals were doing on RISE. Ten of 11 interviewed principals commented positively on the changes to the rubric, including one who said, "The changes better reflect the time allocation of what they are asking us to do, especially RISE and working with teachers on improvement plans. They took out a lot of the fluff."

Principals had expressed some concerns about the rubric and evaluation process in earlier years, and these concerns continued to be salient through year 4. In particular, less than one-quarter of principal survey respondents agreed or strongly agreed that the process was applied consistently by all assistant superintendents. The small fraction of respondents reporting consistency of rubric application, which was also observed in year 3, indicates concern among principals in the area of rubric interrater agreement. When we asked assistant superintendents whether they had regularly engaged in professional development related to establishing consistency of rubric use, we were told that, in the first year of PPIP, assistant superintendents met regularly with an outside adviser and received support and coaching on their evaluation of principals. In later years, however, assistant superintendents said that they did not engage in regular, intensive professional development (e.g., in the form of dedicated assistant superintendent meetings or workshops with external consultants) regarding use of the rubric or to address questions of interrater agreement.

Of course, because each assistant superintendent works with a specific type of school (e.g., high schools, K–8 schools, K–5 schools), there may be legitimate reasons for some differences in expectations regarding evidence. But interviews revealed perceptions among principals that some assistant superintendents are "easier" raters than others, which suggests that there might be additional between-rater differences that go beyond responding to the specific context in which principals work. In addition to concerns about interrater agreement, a few other findings in Table 4.2 suggest areas

Table 4.2
Principals' Opinions of the Administrators' Performance Standard Rubric, Year 4

Response	Agree/Strongly Agree (%)
The rubric evaluation process has helped me think about my leadership strengths and weaknesses	86
The targets I need to meet (i.e., ratings of "proficient" or "accomplished") are realistic	76
I have a clear understanding of what I need to do in order to achieve a salary increase	58
The district is providing the resources and support I need to meet the targets required to earn a salary increase	40
The performance evaluation process using the Administrators' Performance Standard Rubric is fair to all principals in PPS, regardless of the type of school in which they work	39
I have altered how I allocate my time toward the leadership tasks emphasized on the rubric	38
The rubric does a good job of distinguishing effective from ineffective principals in PPS	37
The online system for collecting rubric evidence has significantly reduced the paperwork burden	37
The rubric evaluation process is applied consistently by all of the assistant superintendents	23
Collecting rubric documentation requires an excessive amount of paperwork	66
The Administrators' Performance Standard Rubric contains so many standards and components that I can't possibly address all of them	38
It will be relatively difficult for me to earn a salary increase this year because conditions in my school prevent me from engaging in the practices specified by the rubric	16
The rubric evaluation process has negatively affected my relationship with my assistant superintendent	8

NOTE: The survey item read, "To what extent do you agree or disagree with the following statements about the Administrators' Performance Standard Rubric that is used to determine salary increments? As a reminder, the first three standards of the rubric changed at the beginning of the 2010–2011 school year." Principals who did not participate in the rubric-based evaluation the previous year were instructed to skip this item. Sample sizes ranged from 49 to 52. Responses were given on a scale of 1 = strongly disagree, 2 = disagree, 3 = agree, and 4 = strongly agree. Responses are sorted in descending order by percentage responding "agree" or "strongly agree." Negatively worded items, shown in shaded rows, are grouped and sorted separately from positively worded items.

that might need to be addressed: Only 37 percent indicated that the rubric did a good job distinguishing effective from ineffective principals, and 39 percent reported that the evaluation process was fair to all principals in PPS, regardless of the type of school in which they worked. These responses suggest that many principals are skeptical of the validity of the rubric.

Large majorities of principals expressed skepticism about the validity of the bonus measure. Table 4.3 shows that principals had concerns about the bonus, but their opinions were not uniformly negative. Only one-third of survey respondents reported negative effects on principal morale, and even fewer indicated negative effects on principals' willingness to collaborate. Moreover, the fact that only 38 percent agreed or strongly agreed with the statement "Rewarding individual principals based on test score gains is problematic because the principal has limited control over student learning in the school" suggests that most principals were not opposed to achievement-based rewards in principle. Agreement with this statement declined over time in the linked data: Sixty-nine percent agreed or strongly agreed in year 2, compared with 46 percent in year 3 and 39 percent in year 4 (a statistically significant change; see Appendix D, Table D.21). Inspection of the responses for all principals (not just those in the linked

Table 4.3
Principals' Opinions of the Achievement Bonus, Year 4

Response	Agree/Strongly Agree (%)
District staff have communicated about how the achievement bonus is calculated in a way that is clear and understandable to me	31
The district is providing the resources and support I need to meet the targets required to earn a bonus	29
The PPIP method of awarding bonuses is fair to all principals in PPS, regardless of the type of school in which they work	23
The PPIP method of awarding bonuses does a good job of distinguishing effective from ineffective principals in PPS	10
I have not altered my practices as a result of the prospect of earning a bonus	68
Rewarding individual principals based on test score gains is problematic because the principal has limited control over student learning in the school	38
The bonus program has negatively affected principals' morale	33
The bonus program has negatively affected principals' willingness to collaborate	14

NOTE: The survey item read, "To what extent do you agree or disagree with the following statements about the *achievement bonus* component of PPIP?" Sample sizes ranged from 51 to 53. Responses were given on a scale of 1 = strongly disagree, 2 = disagree, 3 = agree, and 4 = strongly agree. Responses are sorted in descending order by percentage responding "agree" or "strongly agree." Negatively worded items, shown in shaded rows, are grouped and sorted separately from positively worded items.

sample) showed a similar decline over time (see Appendix D, Table D.20, for year 3 bonus data).

However, more than three-quarters of principals in year 4 still expressed concerns about fairness, and only 10 percent reported that the bonus did a good job of distinguishing effective from ineffective principals. These findings were reinforced by the interviews. None of the principals who participated in the interviews described the bonus in positive terms, and, regardless of the type of school in which a principal worked, most principals said they believed that the bonus favored schools unlike their own. To illustrate, one principal in a low-income school said that principals received the bonus only if they worked "in a nice middle-class school," while another said that the bonus was "impossible to earn if you are in a school that is already performing decently." The interviews indicated that many principals still did not understand how the bonus was calculated, a finding that is reinforced by the survey results summarized in Table 4.3. In addition, all of the principals who were interviewed reported not being motivated by money; one said, "I'm embarrassed by it. As a professional you shouldn't need that extra carrot." It is worth noting that, as shown in Table 4.3, most principals reported not altering their practices in response to the bonus. If these findings accurately reflect principals' behavioral responses to the bonus, the finding suggests that pay-for-performance policies alone are unlikely to lead to significant changes in practice. This finding is consistent with recent studies that have found little or no effect of performance pay for teachers on instructional practices or student outcomes (Springer, Pane, et al., forthcoming; Springer, Ballou, et al., 2010; Marsh et al., 2011).

Principals' responses to PPIP interventions were unrelated to the characteristics of their schools, with a few exceptions. Our ability to detect differences in principals' responses by school and principal characteristics was limited by our small sample sizes. We did, however, conduct a set of exploratory correlational analyses to examine relationships between principals' survey responses and school characteristics. We relied on the survey scales rather than individual items because the scales have less measurement error and therefore enhance our likelihood of detecting relationships.

We examined relationships with the following survey scales: contribution of professional development to professional growth, perceived effects of Leadership Academy professional development, assistant superintendent support for instructional leadership, assistant superintendent support for general (noninstructional) leadership, and opinions about the rubric (see Appendix A, published separately, for a description of these scales). The full correlation matrix for this analysis appears as Table E.1 in Appendix E (published separately; it also includes a set of scales we examine in Chapter Five). We found significant correlations for two of these scales, though these need to be interpreted cautiously because we did not adjust the significance level for multiple comparisons and because they provide no information about whether the relationship is causal or whether it stems from some other factor that we did not measure. Principals' opinions about the value of Leadership Academy professional development were negatively associated with the percentage of students receiving FRL (r = −0.28) and positively associated with the percentage of gifted students in the school (r = 0.26). Principals' opinions about the rubric were negatively associated with the percentage of students receiving FRL (r = −0.28) and with the percentage of students with limited English proficiency (LEP) in the school (r = 0.41). Although assistant superintendents told us they provided more support to schools with greater needs, we did not observe significant correlations between principals' opinions about this support and school characteristics. In Chapter Six, we examine the extent to which principals' views measured by these scales are associated with their performance on the rubric.

Because the principal survey items addressing opinions about the achievement bonus did not lend themselves to a scale, we also examined the relationships between school characteristics and selected individual survey questions about the achievement bonus. Table E.2 in Appendix E presents these correlations. Principal perceptions about whether the bonus was fair to principals regardless of the type of school in which they worked were not associated with school characteristics. However, principals who worked in schools with more gifted students (r = 0.34), with fewer students receiving FRL (r = −0.25), and with students from neighborhoods with higher adult educational attainment (r = 0.35) were more likely to report that the bonus formula did a good job distinguishing between more and less effective principals. In addition, principals of schools with fewer African American students were more likely to agree that principals had limited control over student learning (r = −0.34). In Chapter Six, we examine the extent to which principals' views as measured by these survey questions were associated with their achievement bonus.

Most principals were unaware of the premium for working in high-need schools or did not view it as an incentive to work in those schools. The survey asked principals whether they were aware that principals who worked in high-need schools were eligible to receive a premium as part of their bonuses. Approximately half of respondents (48 percent) responded yes; the remaining principals responded no. The principals who reported being aware of the premium were then asked to indicate their level of agreement with the statement "The high-need bonus premium is an incentive for principals to work in high-need schools." Only 21 percent of respondents agreed or strongly agreed with this statement, and 48 percent strongly disagreed. These findings suggest that both lack of awareness and lack of enthusiasm for the premium may be preventing this part of the initiative from having its intended effect.

Summary of Key Findings

The results described in this chapter indicate that principals valued many of the capacity-building interventions that the district provided. At the same time, principals expressed concerns about the measures used to evaluate their performance, and they are particularly skeptical about the validity and fairness of the bonus measure. In addition, principals continued to assert that they were not motivated by financial incentives. These findings regarding principals' attitudes are important because these attitudes are likely to influence the long-term success of the interventions adopted under PPIP, but they do not tell us whether the program has influenced what principals do or what happens in their schools. In Chapter Five, we address these outcomes by examining principals' perceptions of changes in their leadership skills and practices.

Principals' Leadership Practices, Principals' Skills, and School- and Classroom-Level Responses to the Pittsburgh Principal Incentive Program

As outlined in the program's TOA described in Chapter Three, PPIP is meant to achieve its goals by providing capacity-building interventions to build principals' skills and by shifting the focus of principals' time and attention in ways that lead to improved instruction and student achievement. This chapter describes how principals' practices and skills changed over the course of PPIP implementation, and it explores ways in which those changes in principals appear to be influencing instruction and learning in their schools.

Changes in Principals' Leadership Practices and Skills

The professional development and other PPIP supports, as well as the design of the Administrators' Performance Standard Rubric, were intended to help principals identify the areas in which they needed to improve their skills and to help them prioritize among the various tasks that comprise their work as school leaders. In this section, we examine the extent to which principals report changes in their practices and skills, and we provide some corroborating evidence from coaches and other school staff.

Principals' Practices
PPS principals have spent significantly more time observing and evaluating teachers and providing feedback on instruction since PPIP was put in place. The PPIP rubric promoted a focus of the principal evaluation system on the principal's role as instructional leader, and the district's Leadership Academy professional development and coaching from the assistant superintendents further encouraged and supported that focus. Data from principal and coach surveys show that, during PPIP, principals reportedly spent more of their time in classrooms than they did prior to implementation of PPIP. This outcome is clearly aligned with PPIP's TOA; however, other elements of the district's overall strategy to improve teaching effectiveness that were implemented subsequent to PPIP—particularly RISE—probably also contributed to this shift.

In years 2–4 of PPIP, the principal survey included a list of ten or more core principal tasks, asking respondents to estimate how many hours they spent on each task in a typical week. Figure 5.1 shows the percentage of principals in each year who said they spent more than ten hours per week observing in teachers' classrooms and providing feedback—an amount of time consistent with the level the district was encouraging through PPIP training and coaching.

Some of this increase in principal time in classrooms appears to have been due to a change in the principal pool (not coincidentally, another aspect of the PPIP strategy). Specifically, most principals who began their tenure during PPIP participated in the PELA program, the district's training program for new administrators (see Chapter Three for a description). Two of the goals of the PELA program were to establish the expectation among new principals that they will spend a significant amount of time in classrooms working with teachers on instruction and to provide new principals with experience observing teachers and providing feedback. When looking at the smaller number of principals (n = 21) who responded to this survey item in all three years, we see a more pronounced version of the same trend, from none of that group spending more than ten hours per week in classrooms in year 2 of the program to 66 percent of those same individuals doing so in year 3 to 67 percent in year 4. This change is also consistent with the duties principals took on as the district began implementing RISE.

Coaches confirmed principal reports of more principal time spent in classrooms. Because PPIP formally encourages and rewards principals for spending more time

Figure 5.1
Changes in Principals' Time Spent Observing in Teachers' Classrooms and Providing Feedback, Years 2–4

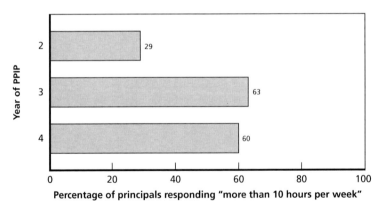

NOTES: The survey item read, "Below is a list of activities that can be part of a principal's job. Thinking about the nature of your work this school year, please estimate how much time you devote to each activity in a typical week." Sample sizes were 35 in year 2, 48 in year 3, and 59 in year 4. Responses were given on a scale of 1 = not done weekly, 2 = 1–4 hours per week, 3 = 5–10 hours per week, 4 = 11–15 hours per week, and 5 = more than 15 hours per week. Responses are sorted in descending order by year.
RAND *MG1223-5.1*

in classrooms, reliance on self-report data (principals reporting that they are doing what the system tells them to do) on principal time allocation is insufficient. However, the finding is strongly confirmed by the year 4 coach survey, in which 89 percent of building-level coaches reported that their principals were spending more time observing teachers and providing feedback than they had in the previous year. More than 80 percent of coaches agreed that their principals visited classrooms at least three times per week and that the amount of time their principals spent in classrooms was "appropriate." Additionally, the percentage of all coaches who agreed that their principals visit classrooms at least three times per week increased from 76 percent in year 3 to 89 percent in year 4, a finding that is consistent with principals' own reports of spending more time in this area.

In addition to informal classroom observations, principals reported spending significant amounts of additional time working with teachers on their instruction. Forty percent of principals in year 3 and 45 percent in year 4 reported spending more than ten hours per week conducting formal evaluations of teachers. A smaller but nontrivial number of principals (26 percent in year 3, 20 percent in year 4) reported spending more than ten hours per week working with teachers on improvement plans. Those principals who had teachers on improvement plans reported that working with them was very time-consuming but that such a process was "long overdue." In interviews, some principals reported feeling that, because of the union contract, only a formal improvement plan allowed them to give struggling teachers the intensive support they needed. In certain cases, in which the principals reported that the support provided to teachers through improvement plans was not well-received or was still not enough, the process allowed them to "get rid of the dead wood."

The additional time principals spent on teacher observations should have resulted in a reduction in time on other activities, unless principals were simply working more hours per week. In interviews, some principals did report working longer hours. However, the survey data show some areas in which principals reported spending less time by year 4 of PPIP (Table 5.1).

Principals may also have carved out more time for instructional leadership through increased delegation. The percentage of principals in the linked data who reported that they spent more than ten hours per week "working with the instructional coaches, ITLs, grade or department leaders, or other instructional leaders in (their) building" increased from 10 percent in years 2 and 3 to 24 percent in year 4. This time spent planning and coordinating may be an investment that allows principals to delegate some tasks to these other instructional leaders. For example, seven of the nine coaches interviewed said that their principals played a productive role in site-based professional development primarily by co-planning it with coaches and grade-level leaders but delegating actual leadership of the sessions. In the year 4 surveys, 69 percent of principals and 83 percent of coaches agreed or strongly agreed that the principal was able to del-

Table 5.1
Areas in Which Principals Report Spending Less Than Ten Hours per Week, Years 3 and 4

Activity	Year 3	Year 4
Supporting curriculum implementation in my building	42	15
Other management issues (budget, personnel, administrative paperwork)	38	29
Developing or leading professional development for staff	21	11
Communicating or interacting with parents or the community	34	27

NOTE: This table shows yearly totals, not linked data.

egate some management tasks to others, thus perhaps enabling them to spend more time on higher-priority areas.

Principals' Perceptions of Their Skills and Need for Support

Not only were principals spending more time observing and providing feedback on instruction, but this was also the area in which they believed that their skills had grown most under PPIP. In addition to questions about time allocation, we also collected data from principals and coaches regarding perceptions of principal skills in various leadership domains. On the year 4 survey, principals were asked in which two of 14 possible leadership skills they had grown the most since PPIP was first implemented (or since joining the district if they joined after PPIP began). Only three areas were selected by more than ten principals as a top growth area, and all three had to do with working with teachers on instruction, as shown in Figure 5.2.

Conversely, the domains that principals selected as those in which they would most like to have more training and support suggest areas in which principals still felt they could develop their skills. Five skill areas were selected by at least nine principals as among the top two areas in which they would like more training and support (Table 5.2).

This pattern of self-reported strengths and areas of need suggests that PPIP's emphasis on instructional leadership, in combination with the specific requirements of RISE implementation, have built principals' confidence in their ability to observe and evaluate instruction. Other areas of instructional leadership, including curriculum support and data use, remain areas of opportunity for leadership growth.

Other Staff Perceptions of Principals' Leadership

Most coaches rated their principals' leadership as effective, with particularly strong agreement that they were effective in the areas of providing professional development opportunities, giving feedback on instruction, and helping teachers use data. In year 4 of the evaluation, 75 to 80 percent of coaches in PPS agreed or strongly agreed that their principals were effective across a wide range of leadership domains, including the instructional

Figure 5.2
Number of Principal Survey Respondents Indicating Areas in Which Skills Improved the Most Since the Pittsburgh Principal Incentive Program Was First Implemented, Year 4

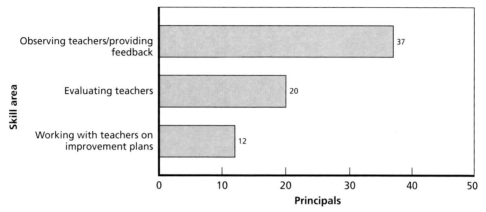

NOTE: The survey item read, "Area in which my leadership skills have grown the most since PPIP. (Select up to two.)" Sample size is 52. Responses are sorted in descending order by number of principals choosing that response. Principals were instructed to select up to two areas in which their skills had grown the most since PPIP from a list of 14.

RAND *MG1223-5.2*

Table 5.2
Number of Principal Survey Respondents Indicating Areas in Which They Would Like to See Pittsburgh Public Schools Provide More Training and Support, Year 4

Selected Area	Principals
Supporting curriculum implementation	22
Reviewing student achievement data with staff[a]	16
Handling student discipline issues	10
Developing or leading professional development for staff	9
Communicating with parents and the community	9

NOTE: N = 57. Responses are sorted in descending order by number of principals identifying that area. Principals were instructed to select up to two areas in which they would like more support and training from a list of 14.

[a] Note that only three principals indicated a desire for further training on "reviewing student achievement data myself," suggesting that it is not the analytical skills on which they feel they could improve but how to use data most productively in working with their staff.

leadership tasks encouraged by PPIP and the district's overall improvement strategy.[1] Figure 5.3 shows the percentage of coaches who agree or strongly agree that their principals have each of the several instructional leadership skills.

Although there was little variation in the percentage of total agreement, the percentage of coaches agreeing strongly with each statement gives a more nuanced perspective on leadership strengths. In general, coaches' assessment is congruent with how the principals assessed their own skills, particularly in the identification of curriculum knowledge as an area of relative weakness.

The number of coaches who strongly agreed that their principals provided teachers with useful feedback on instruction rose from 22 percent in year 3 to 37 percent in year 4. In interviews, coaches attributed this change largely to RISE, noting that RISE has given principals a structure for providing teaches with more-targeted and, thus, more-useful feedback.

Large majorities of teachers described their administrators as strong and supportive instructional leaders. The 2010–2011 Intensive Partnership Sites evaluation teacher

Figure 5.3
Coach Survey Respondents' Assessments of Principals' Instructional Leadership Skills, Year 4

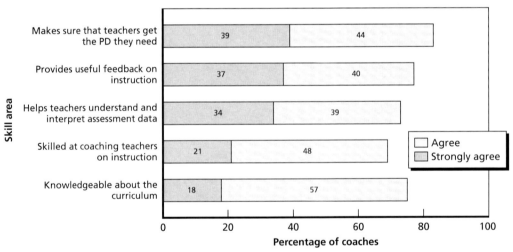

NOTE: The survey item read, "Please indicate your level of agreement or disagreement with the following statements. The principal in my building . . . ." Sample sizes ranged from 57 to 60. Responses are sorted in descending order by percentage responding that they "strongly agree." Responses were given on a scale of 1 = strongly disagree, 2 = disagree, 3 = agree, and 4 = strongly agree.
RAND *MG1223-5.3*

---

[1] Factor analysis of the coach survey data revealed that coaches' ratings of their principals' effectiveness tended to be consistent across a wide array of skills. Coaches found their principals either generally effective or generally ineffective, rather than being effective in some areas and ineffective in others. In the view of coaches, then, PPS has a small number of principals who are perceived as ineffective across the board as opposed to a large number of principals with specific development needs.

survey (administered in year 4 of PPIP) asked teachers a set of questions about administrators in their schools. In many cases, teachers' responses reflect teachers' assessments of the principals, as well as other school leaders, but the responses provide a window into the extent to which the principal is providing leadership that supports teachers' efforts to promote student learning. The results, shown in Figure 5.4, suggest widespread satisfaction among teachers for the quality of administrators' leadership. Ninety percent of teachers agreed or strongly agreed that their administrators were highly focused on student learning, and 75 percent agreed or strongly agreed that administrators were highly supportive of teachers and that respondents viewed their principals as instructional leaders. Although these data were collected for a different purpose, they provide evidence to corroborate principal and coach reports about principals' leadership.

Perceived Role of the Pittsburgh Principal Incentive Program
In year 4, principals were more likely to attribute changes in their practice to RISE than to PPIP. As noted previously, it is difficult to isolate the causal impact of PPIP from other district strategies. Although this creates a challenge for evaluating PPIP, it is consistent with the district's goal of ensuring that the various reforms are aligned and working

Figure 5.4
Teacher Survey Respondents' Assessments of School Administrators, Year 4

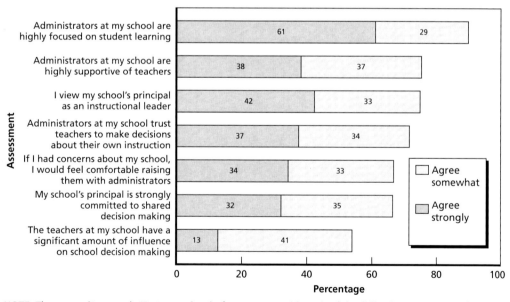

NOTE: The survey item read, "Rate your level of agreement with each of the following statements about your school." Sample is 657. Responses are sorted in descending order by the sum of "agree" and "strongly agree." Responses were given on a scale of 1 = strongly disagree, 2 = disagree, 3 = agree, and 4 = strongly agree.
RAND MG1223-5.4

toward common goals. When asked directly, principals were reluctant to attribute any change in their practice to PPIP and were particularly reluctant to attribute changes in their practice to the financial incentives. Among 11 principals interviewed this year, three had been principals only under PPIP and could make no comparison with their pre-PPIP practice. Six of the remaining eight said that PPIP had no direct impact on their practice. The other two cited the general impact that the PPIP rubric gives them a framework for thinking about leadership or the allocation of their time as leaders. Overall, in interviews, principals were much more likely to connect specific practice changes to requirements of the RISE program. In that context, however, several principals noted that the programs reinforce each other: "PPIP is not that specific, but combined with the RISE rubric, *yes*! I have changed how I work with teachers."

School- and Classroom-Level Changes

Of course, these reported changes in principals' skills and time allocation are not ends in themselves. The PPIP TOA posits that these changes will pay off in classroom-level changes and instructional improvement in the schools these principals lead and, ultimately, contribute to improved student achievement. This section describes the use of three district-encouraged instructional improvement strategies (in-school professional development, data use, and incorporation of TLT feedback) and the extent to which they were evident at the classroom level.

In-School Professional Development

Principals took an active role in site-specific professional development. Our school-level interviews indicated strong principal involvement in site-level professional development, as encouraged by PPIP. Of nine principal/coach pairs, seven coaches stated that their principals played a productive role in site-based professional development, mostly by co-planning it with the coach.[2] Actual leading of professional development sessions was often delegated to coaches, which is one factor that helps explain why fewer principals reported spending more than ten hours per week developing and leading professional development in year 4 than in year 3 (see Table 5.1). At the same time, many coaches reported that principals were more likely to attend and participate in professional development than in earlier years of PPIP. In the year 4 coach survey, 44 percent of coaches reported that their principals spent more time leading professional development for staff than in the previous year, 11 percent reported that their principal spent less time, and 42 percent reported no change.

---

[2]   In the other two cases, one coach reported—and the principal confirmed—that the principal was not actively involved in site-level professional development. At the other extreme, one coach reported that the principal was overinvolved and often led sessions perceived by teachers to be "superficial busywork."

In the year 4 surveys, 81 percent of principals and 79 percent of coaches agreed that their school-level professional development was well aligned to specific school needs. When we unpack this number, however, it appears that there were emerging concerns among principals about control over and alignment of site-level professional-development time, with overall agreement dropping somewhat and strong agreement dropping sharply between years 3 and 4 (Figure 5.5).

Strong agreement with this item dropped among coaches as well in year 4. Interviews suggested that this change was, at least in part, a result of the district-wide roll-out of RISE in year 4 of PPIP. During that year, the focus of school-level professional development was the rollout of the RISE process and components rather than school-specific instructional improvement efforts. Once RISE is well-established, principals may be able to devote more of their school-level professional development to site-specific needs.

Figure 5.5
Principal Survey Respondents' Assessments of Alignment of Professional Development with School Needs, Years 3 and 4

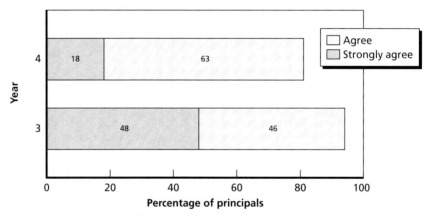

NOTE: The survey item read, "Please indicate your level of agreement about instructional improvement efforts in your school during the current school year." Sample sizes were 46 in year 3 and 60 in year 4. Responses are sorted in descending order by year. Responses were given on a scale of 1 = strongly disagree, 2 = disagree, 3 = agree, and 4 = strongly agree.
RAND *MG1223-5.5*

Incorporating Data into Instructional Leadership

Most principals were active data users. In the year 4 coach survey, 73 percent of coaches agreed that their principals "[help] teachers understand and interpret assessment data." In interviews, seven of nine coaches described their principals as active data users and confirmed that data in some form are used at most staff meetings. At the other two schools, coaches reported that their principals used data only "in crisis mode" or "to find the bubble kids." At the seven schools where coaches described principals as active data users, principal/coach pairs, when interviewed separately, painted congruent pictures of routine data use, usually including data walls or binders. As was the case in year 3, respondents working in schools at all grade levels spoke of the unexpected benefits of having students more aware of their own data. Respondents in year 4 were more likely than those in year 3 to describe data being used to design and target interventions.

The interview data collected over the course of this study have shown a consistent trend of school-level data use becoming more frequent, more consistent, and more in-depth (e.g., school staff using more-varied data sources and drilling down to more-specific levels). The year 4 surveys showed some decline in agreement among principals and coaches that their teachers not only had the skills and knowledge to use data effectively but were also regularly using data for instructional decision making (Table 5.3). The reason for these declines is not clear.

These declines are from high levels of agreement, however, and more than 65 percent of coaches and principals continued to report regular and skilled use of data by their teachers in year 4.

Table 5.3
Principal and Coach Survey Respondents' Assessments of Teachers' Data Use, Years 3 and 4

| Statement | Percentage Agreeing or Strongly Agreeing | | | |
| | Coaches | | Principals | |
	Year 3	Year 4	Year 3	Year 4
Most teachers in this school use data for instructional decision making on a regular basis	71	72	88	66
Most teachers in this school have the necessary knowledge and skills to use data effectively	85	72	89	69

NOTE: Principal sample sizes were 46 in year 3 and 61 in year 4. Coach sample sizes were 73 in year 3 and 58 in year 4. Responses were given on a scale of 1 = strongly disagree, 2 = disagree, 3 = agree, and 4 = strongly agree.

Teaching and Learning Teams

Year 4 data were mixed on the value of TLTs as a means of site-level instructional improvement. On the positive side, the new "problem-of-practice" approach was well received:[3] In the schools where this approach was used, both principals and coaches reported that this approach made the visits more relevant to school-specific issues and helped TLT members focus the expertise of team members on the specific issues at hand, some-

---

[3]   In the problem-of-practice approach, principals identified an instructional issue or problem for which they wanted feedback, such as a teacher who was having difficulty with questioning techniques, and solicited suggestions for improvement from the TLT.

thing that had been a challenge in the past. The new approach, with its negotiated focus, also contributed to principals and coaches seeing the visits as more collaborative and supportive. On the negative side, principals and coaches found little support for implementation of next steps recommended by the TLT, and principals and coaches at only six of the 11 schools in our interview set for year 4 reported implementing any of those next steps. Survey data support these accounts. In year 4, 63 percent of principals agreed or strongly agreed that TLT next steps were specific enough to act on, but just 46 percent of principals agreed or strongly agreed that TLT input had been a major influence on their instructional improvement efforts. The fact that only 24 percent of principals agreed or strongly agreed that TLT next steps were followed by support for implementation may explain the lack of site-level impact. All of these principal survey ratings on TLT utility—from specificity to influence to follow-up—were lower in year 4 than in year 3 (Figure 5.6).

Figure 5.6
Principal Survey Respondents' Opinions Regarding Teaching and Learning Team Visits, Years 3 and 4

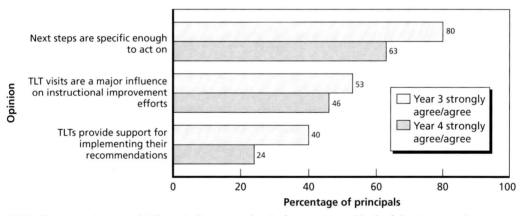

NOTE: The survey item read, "Please indicate your level of agreement with the following questions about TLT visits to your school during the current school year." Sample sizes were 44–45 in year 3 and 49–51 in year 4. Responses are sorted in descending order by year 4 agreement. Responses were given on a scale of 1 = strongly disagree, 2 = disagree, 3 = agree, and 4 = strongly agree.
RAND MG1223-5.6

Changes in Classrooms

The data reported in the previous section suggest that principals were making the kinds of focused investments in instructional improvement that PPIP was designed to promote. The biggest changes, supported not only by PPIP but also by RISE and the district's overall focus on improving teacher effectiveness (e.g., through the EET program), are in the amount of time principals spent observing and coaching teachers and the skill with which they evidently did so. Our results also suggest that, in most schools, data use had become a stronger component of school-level instructional improvement efforts over the period of PPIP implementation. The impacts of site-specific professional development and TLT visits as principals' tools for instructional leadership were more varied, with some schools finding these tools helpful and well aligned with their school improvement agendas, and other schools finding them less helpful.

The bottom line is this: To what extent do these investments show up in classrooms? In the principal survey, we asked principals directly about whether they see "specific evidence" of these instructional improvement strategies when they are observing in classrooms. Figure 5.7 shows the percentage of principals and coaches who reported seeing specific evidence that three major instructional improvement investments, principal feedback, site-specific professional development, and use of data for instructional decision making, were used in the classroom.

Principal and coach reports of classroom evidence of each instructional improvement strategy were at similar levels in years 3 and 4 of the study. Confidence in principal reports of classroom implementation of instructional improvement efforts is strengthened by the fact that coaches' responses to the same items are very similar, although principals are more likely to report seeing their own feedback being used.

In the year 4 interviews, principal/coach pairs (n = 9) were asked an open-ended question about changes they observed in teachers' instructional practice ("Are teachers teaching differently because of any of the things we've been talking about?"). All interviewed principals described improvements in teaching, but there were few consis-

Figure 5.7
Principal and Coach Survey Respondents' Reports of Evidence Observed in Classrooms, Year 4

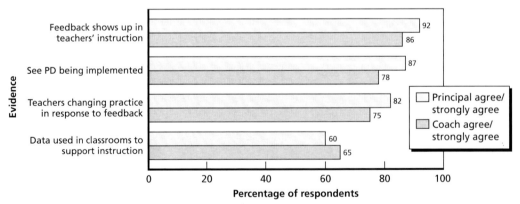

NOTE: The survey item for principals read, "Please indicate your level of agreement about instructional improvement efforts in your school during the current school year (2010–2011)." The survey item for coaches read, "Please indicate your level of agreement about data use and professional development in your school during the current school year (2010–2011)." Sample sizes for principals ranged from 59 to 61 and for coaches from 55 to 59. Responses are sorted in descending order by percentage of principal agreement. Responses were given on a scale of 1 = strongly disagree, 2 = disagree, 3 = agree, and 4 = strongly agree.
RAND *MG1223-5.7*

tent themes across schools: Four mentioned improved questioning techniques, three mentioned more-effective data use, three cited more-rigorous classroom discussions, and three mentioned more collaboration among teachers around instruction. Among coaches, two reported no change in teaching practice. Of the other seven, four saw more data use and two saw more collaboration. At four of the nine schools where interviews were conducted, the coach's answer was consistent with the principal's answer in terms of the specific instructional change named.

Principals and coaches across schools agreed in describing increased levels of student engagement in and ownership of their own learning. Principal/coach interviewee pairs were asked about changes they observed in student learning related to the various instructional improvement strategies. All nine principals and seven of nine coaches reported positive changes.[4] Although descriptions of changed teaching practice varied in their specifics, descriptions of changes in student learning were very consistent both between principals and coaches and across schools: Interviewees described students at their school as more engaged, more active in their own learning, and more aware of their own performance data and how specifically they could improve.

Principals' perceptions of the quality of instructional improvement efforts and leadership support in their schools were associated with school demographic characteristics. Table E.1 in Appendix E, published separately, shows correlations between school characteristics and four principal survey scales related to principal practices and school- and classroom-level responses: principal time spent on instructional leadership, principal time spent on management, opinions about instructional improvement efforts, and opinions about TLTs. Three of the four scales showed no significant relationships with school characteristics. However, responses to the instructional improvement scale, which measures principals' perceptions regarding teacher capacity, teacher practices, and quality of instructional leadership teams, were more positive for principals serving schools with fewer students moving into PPS from other districts, fewer African American students, fewer IEP students, and greater percentages of students from affluent neighborhoods.

Summary

During the four years of PPIP implementation, principal time allocation and skills appear to have grown in the kinds of hands-on instructional leadership supported and

---

[4] The two coaches who reported seeing no change in student learning at their school were the same two who saw no change in teaching practice. One coach commented, "Anything is a temporary fix: 'Next time the TLT comes I will do x,' but it doesn't really become part of practice. Teachers in this building are not open to change." Earlier, when asked about how the principal coaches teachers on instruction, this same coach reported, "Practice is not open—[principals] can't come in informally and offer feedback. That is the culture of the school: Teachers don't want [principals] in the room."

rewarded by the program. Principals were clearly spending more time in classrooms working with teachers on their instruction, and large majorities of coaches reported that teachers value this principal feedback. Other aspects of the district's reform approach, particularly RISE, supported principal growth in the skills of classroom observation and feedback. Changes in instructional leadership during PPIP implementation were not limited to increased principal presence in classrooms and confidence in their instructional coaching skills. Principals were providing time, structure, and direct support for instructional data use, and all schools in our interview set reported increased frequency and depth of instructional data use during the past four years. Principals also became more involved in developing professional development specific to site improvement needs, although, in year 4, a great deal of professional development time at the site was devoted to district-determined RISE issues.

CHAPTER SIX

Principals' Performance on Rubric and Achievement Measures

As discussed in Chapter Three, PPIP includes two compensation components: an increment of up to $2,000 that is added to principals' base salary and a bonus of up to $10,000. The amount of increment in base salary depends on a principal's performance on the evaluation rubric, his or her tenure as a PPS principal, and the AYP status of his or her school. The bonus amount is based on his or her school's performance on the achievement measures in a given school year and, starting in year 3, the high-need status of his or her school. This chapter presents descriptive information on principals' performance on both measures.

We present several analyses that explore principals' performance on the rubric, including relationships with selected principal and school characteristics. We then present findings related to principals' performance on the achievement bonus measure. We focus on the final year of the program, in which we expect to see the greatest impact, but also comment on differences from earlier years. We comment on changes over time and explore whether our findings seem to be transitory or whether they reflect fundamental characteristics of the performance measures. We also examine whether either the rubric scores or the achievement bonus measures are associated with principals' responses to the scales we created from the survey items.

Of perhaps greatest interest is whether there is evidence of a relationship between performance on the rubric and achievement growth. In years 2 and 3, we found some evidence of a positive relationship between rubric performance and achievement growth. For the first time, in year 4, we find a large positive and statistically significant correlation between principals' performance as measured by the rubric and student mathematics achievement growth in the same year. This finding suggests that PPS is measuring and rewarding behaviors with the rubric that are associated with achievement growth.

Principals' Performance on the Evaluation Rubric

The rubric that assistant superintendents used to evaluate principals' performance in year 4 included five standards and reflected a research-based understanding of the leadership qualities and practices that have been positively associated with student learning (see Chapter Three). In this section, we present some descriptive information on principals' performance on the rubric. The analyses presented here include the 42 principals who were evaluated on the rubric in year 4. Most of the other principals participated in DPG projects, per the scheduled rotation. In addition, a small number of principals not evaluated on the rubric were on improvement plans. The principals on improvement plans were so placed because of performance issues detected by their assistant superintendents, either prior to the beginning of the year or during the year. All principals who were on the rubric were rated as "satisfactory" on their formal personnel evaluations. It is important to keep in mind when examining correlations with the rubric that the lowest-performing principals are not included in those calculations, leading to a restriction of range that is likely to depress the magnitudes of the correlations to some degree.

According to the rating protocol for the rubric in year 4 of PPIP, each principal received a score ranging from 1 to 4 on each of 22 components. A rating of 1 indicated rudimentary performance, 2 indicated emerging, 3 was proficient, and 4 was accomplished. These 22 components were clustered into five standards; standards 1, 3, and 5 consisted of five components each; standard 2 had four components, and standard 4 had three. For each component, scoring at the proficient or accomplished level was viewed as meeting the criteria. For each standard, a principal was considered to be meeting the standard if he or she scored at least proficient on each of the components included in that standard.

For the analyses presented in this chapter, we computed three types of summary scores for each principal. The first is the sum of individual ratings on each of the components. The second is the number of components on which the principal met the criteria (proficient or accomplished). The third is the number of standards each principal met. The ranges of these summary scores vary depending on the number of components and standards evaluated each year, so we also report a percentage of the maximum possible in each year. These various ways of summarizing the scores provide slightly different information about principal performance, although, as expected, they are all highly correlated with one another. Table 6.1 provides a summary of scores obtained by the 42 principals for whom complete data were available in year 4 of the program.

Average performance on the rubric has not changed over the years. The results in Table 6.1 show the average and variation in principals' scores. The year 4 average of 66.2 is almost exactly equivalent to an average score of three out of four on each component. This is very similar to averages in previous years.

The distribution of rubric scores became more compressed over the life of the program. As was the case in years 2 and 3, the rudimentary rating was not used at all for principals who remained on the rubric in year 4, a finding that is consistent with the fact that the lowest-performing principals were removed from the rubric evaluation process.

Table 6.1
Distributions of Principals' Scores on Rubric, Years 1–4

Score	Mean Score		Standard Deviation		Minimum Score		Maximum Score	
	Value	%	Value	%	Value	%	Value	%
Year 1 (N = 55)								
Total score (108 possible)	74.2	69	19.3	27	27	25	108	100
Number of components at least proficient (27 possible)	19.2	71	8.6	32	0	0	27	100
Number of standards met (i.e., all components at least proficient) (7 possible)	3.7	52	2.5	36	0	0	7	100
Year 2 (N = 37)								
Total score (108 possible)	75.9	70	12.5	12	54	50	104	96
Number of components at least proficient (27 possible)	18.4	68	8.2	30	0	0	27	100
Number of standards met (i.e., all components at least proficient) (7 possible)	3.4	49	2.7	39	0	0	7	100
Year 3 (N = 31)								
Total score (108 possible)	81.4	75	8.1	8	67	62	103	95
Number of components at least proficient (27 possible)	23.5	87	3.9	14	13	48	27	100
Number of standards met (i.e., all components at least proficient) (7 possible)	4.9	70	2.0	29	1	14	7	100
Year 4 (N = 42)								
Total score (88 possible)	66.2	75	6.4	7	51	58	80	91
Number of components at least proficient (22 possible)	19.1	87	3.4	15	7	32	22	100
Number of standards met (i.e., all components at least proficient) (5 possible)	3.6	72	1.4	28	0	0	5	100

At the low end of those scored, the score of 51 is equivalent to an average score of 2.3 out of 4, which is higher than in years 1 and 2. At the other end of the distribution, the highest score of 80 is equivalent to a score of 3.6 out of 4 on the components, which was lower than in previous years. The standard deviation of the total score in year 4 is 6.4, or slightly less than 0.3 on a four-point scale. This is approximately the same as in year 3 but is lower than in years 1 or 2, providing further evidence that the distribution of rubric scores became more compressed over time.

One reason for the compression of the rubric score distribution is a ceiling effect in the rating scale. The number of components on which principals were rated at least proficient ranged from seven to all 22. The average number of standards met (i.e., the number of standards for which principals scored at least proficient on all components) was 3.6 out of five. The number of standards met ranged from zero to five, with one principal meeting no standards, one meeting one standard, and 16 principals meeting all five standards. This apparent ceiling effect is similar to, although more extreme than, that was seen in earlier years of the program.

Table 6.2 provides information about principals' performance on each standard in year 4 and illustrates some differences in average performance across the standards. These mean scores and percentages of principals meeting each standard are similar to those from previous years, and, as in previous years, standard 2 (culture of teaching and learning, which includes such activities as data use, curriculum implementation, and differentiated instruction) was the least likely to be met. In most years, it was met by just over half the principals. At the other end of the spectrum, standard 5 (formerly integrity, fairness, and ethics in learning; now high personal and professional standards) was met by more than 80 percent of the principals in year 4, down from previous years. Performance on the other three standards was fairly tightly clustered, with about 75 percent meeting each standard.

Scores on different standards are highly correlated with one another. We examined the relationships among scores on the five standards and the 22 components to assess whether principals who received high scores on one standard or component were likely to receive high scores on other standards or components and to explore whether the rubric measured a common construct or multiple constructs. We calculated bivariate correlations for the sum of component scores nested under each standard and the number of components met (i.e., rated as proficient or accomplished) on each standard.

Table 6.2
Principals' Performance, by Standard, Year 4

Standard	Mean Score	Average Component Score Out of 4 Points	Percentage Meeting Standard
1: Manages human capital	15.5	3.1	69.0
2: Culture of teaching and learning	11.2	2.8	54.8
3: Management of learning	14.9	3.0	76.2
4: Relationships with community	9.0	3.0	76.2
5: High personal and professional standards	15.6	3.1	81.0

NOTE: N = 42. A principal is classified as meeting a standard if he or she scores proficient or accomplished on each component in that standard. Standards 1, 3, and 5 have five components each, for a maximum score of 20. Standard 2 has four components, and standard 4 has three components, for maximums of 16 and 20, respectively.

Tetrachoric correlations were used for analyses of whether a standard was met (i.e., all components were scored at least proficient). We also conducted exploratory factor analyses to examine the extent to which the different subscores (standard or component scores) appear to measure the same construct or whether they cluster into groups that suggest that multiple constructs are being measured.

Table 6.3 shows the correlations among the five standards using the sum of components scores nested under each standard. It shows that scores for the five standards are all positively and highly correlated with one another. However, these correlations have been decreasing over time, which could suggest that assistant superintendents are improving in their ability to distinguish among various principal behaviors or could simply reflect the lower variation in scores among principals. However, as in previous years, the exploratory factor analysis still suggests that the five standards all appear to measure the same broad construct. That is, there is no evidence that some principals systematically do well on one set of standards and other principals systematically do well on a different set. At the same time, the fact that the correlations are not higher indicates that individual principals perform at different levels across the five standards, and reports from principals that the rubric is helpful for identifying strengths and weaknesses (see Chapter Four) suggest that assistant superintendents are making useful distinctions among the standards even though the scores are correlated.

K–5 principals received significantly better ratings on standards 1 and 2 than did principals of schools with other grade configurations (p-value < 0.05). We conducted exploratory analyses to assess whether principals' rubric scores varied by school grade configuration, by ALA classification, and by level of experience. We also examined relationships between rubric scores and the demographic characteristics of the principal's school. None of the findings reported here should be interpreted as suggesting a causal relationship between principal performance and principal or school characteristics; the analyses are purely descriptive.

Table 6.4 compares the performance of principals in each of four grade configuration categories.[1] For the rubric overall, and for each of the five standards, the table indicates the number of components on which the principal scored at least proficient. We examined the statistical significance of the group differences using a standard analysis of variance (ANOVA), though readers should keep in mind that, with a sample size of only 42, the statistical power of these significance tests is low, and some differences that do not reach statistical significance may nonetheless be meaningful.

On average, principals in K–5 schools received more ratings of proficient or accomplished than did principals in other types of schools, while principals in 6–12 schools received the fewest. The pattern was not universal, however. Only the ratings on standard 1 (manages human capital) follow this overall pattern, although K–5 principals

---

[1] There were no principals with schools in the middle school category who were evaluated on the rubric in year 4.

Table 6.3
Bivariate Correlations Among Total Scores on Each Standard, Using the Sum of Scores

Standard	1	2	3	4	5
1: Manages human capital	1.00				
2: Culture of teaching and learning	0.77	1.00			
3: Management of learning	0.60	0.58	1.00		
4: Relationships with community	0.34	0.36	0.18	1.00	
5: High personal and professional standards	0.48	0.35	0.23	0.35	1.00

NOTE: N = 42.

Table 6.4
Average Number of Components for Which Criteria Were Met (scores were at least proficient), by School Grade Configuration

Grade Level		Total*	Standard				
			1*	2*	3	4	5
K–5 (N = 21)	Mean	20.8	5.0	3.7	4.8	2.5	4.8
	Standard deviation	1.9	0.0	1.0	0.5	0.7	0.5
	Minimum	15	5	0	3	1	3
	Maximum	22	5	4	5	3	5
K–8 (N = 10)	Mean	18.1	4.1	2.0	4.2	2.9	4.9
	Standard deviation	3.0	1.0	1.1	1.3	0.3	0.3
	Minimum	13	2	1	2	2	4
	Maximum	22	5	4	5	3	5
High schools (N = 8)	Mean	17.3	3.5	2.3	4.5	2.8	4.3
	Standard deviation	3.1	1.4	1.6	0.8	0.7	1.8
	Minimum	14	2	0	3	1	0
	Maximum	22	5	4	5	3	5
6–12 schools (N = 3)	Mean	15.7	3.3	2.3	4.0	2.3	3.7
	Standard deviation	7.8	2.1	2.1	1.7	1.2	1.2
	Minimum	7	1	0	2	1	3
	Maximum	22	5	4	5	3	5

NOTE: The scores obtained for ALA principals are included in these averages. * = a statistically significant difference across groups (p-value < 0.05).

were highest on standards 2 (culture of teaching and learning) and 3 (management of learning) as well. The differences across groups were statistically significant for the total number of components met and for standards 1 and 2.

The reasons for the differences across grade configurations cannot be determined from these data. In addition to differences in actual principal performance, they could stem from differences in how the assistant superintendents interpreted the evidence and applied the rubric, and they might also reflect differences in the difficulty of meeting the standards in different types of schools. However, it should be noted that the patterns of differences have changed from the previous year, suggesting that inherent difference by school type is an unlikely explanation. Because we cannot determine whether these differences are related to differential validity by school level or inadequate consistency among raters, more investigation of both of these issues is needed.

Novice principals performed significantly worse than experienced principals on the total number of components for which the criteria were met. Table 6.5 provides comparisons between principals in ALA and non-ALA schools and between novice and experienced principals using the district's definition of *novice* (a principal in his or her first two years as principal or with more than two years of experience who is in his or her first year of service to PPS).

In the program's early years, the ALA principals scored lower than the non-ALA principals on several standards. The lower scores for ALA principals could be due to the additional burden of adopting the ALA reform program that these principals were undertaking at the same time that PPIP was beginning. However, Table 6.5 shows that, by year 4, the performance differences between ALA and non-ALA principals are small and not statistically significant.

Throughout the program, novice principals scored lower than experienced principals, and, this year, the difference was statistically significant on the total number of

Table 6.5
Average Number of Components for Which Criteria Were Met (scores of at least proficient) for Accelerated Learning Academy and Non–Accelerated Learning Academy Principals and for Novice and Experienced Principals

Standard	ALA (N = 6)	Non-ALA (N = 36)	Novice (N = 11)	Experienced (N = 31)
Total	18.8	19.2	17.0**	19.9
1	4.5	4.4	4.0	4.5
2	2.7	2.9	2.5	3.1
3	4.5	4.6	3.7***	4.8
4	2.5	2.7	2.4	2.7
5	4.7	4.6	4.5	4.7

NOTE: ** = a statistically significant difference between groups ($p < 0.05$). *** = a statistically significant difference between groups ($p < 0.01$).

components for which the criteria were met and for standard 3 (management of learning). Although not statistically significant in year 4, the number of components met was lower for novice principals on the other four standards as well. This pattern has been seen in most years of the program.

In contrast with earlier years, rubric performance was significantly associated with student characteristics. An additional set of analyses was conducted to examine relationships between rubric scores and the demographic characteristics of the students enrolled in each principal's school. Table 6.6 shows that there was a significant relationship between the rubric scores and school demographic characteristics. This could happen if the assistant superintendents are allowing student characteristics to influence their ratings of principals' performance, or it could simply reflect an uneven distribution of high-performing principals across different types of schools. This relationship was particularly strong for standard 1 (management of human capital), which was newly implemented in year 4. In particular, principals leading schools with more disadvantaged students had lower ratings. The overall rating and the rating on standard 1 were significantly lower for schools with fewer gifted students, more special-needs stu-

Table 6.6
Correlation of Rubric Scores with Student Characteristics, Year 4

Student Characteristic	Total Rating	Standard				
		1	2	3	4	5
Percentage gifted	0.36**	0.34**	0.28	−0.02	0.36**	0.32**
Percentage with an IEP[a]	−0.39**	−0.43**	−0.29	−0.06	−0.32*	−0.32**
Percentage with LEP	0.24	0.22	0.31	0.17	0.17	−0.02
Percentage new to PPS[b]	−0.28	−0.30	−0.29	0.11	−0.12	−0.40*
Percentage switched PPS schools[c]	−0.03	−0.03	−0.04	0.16	−0.29	0.16
Percentage African American	−0.39**	−0.36**	−0.30	−0.33**	−0.23	−0.21
Percentage receiving FRL	−0.45**	−0.44**	−0.41**	−0.20	−0.35**	−0.21
Income[d]	0.30	0.30**	0.31	0.16	0.24	0.07
Adult education[e]	0.40**	0.43**	0.37**	0.06	0.32**	0.22

NOTE: * = statistically significant difference from zero ($p < 0.10$). ** = statistically significant difference from zero ($p < 0.05$).

[a] Existence of an IEP indicates that the student is a special-needs student (nongifted).

[b] Students who were new to PPS in year 4.

[c] Students who attended a different PPS school in year 3 than in year 4.

[d] Average income in the students' home census tracts relative to the federal poverty level (FPL).

[e] Average adult educational attainment in the students' home census tract.

dents, more African American students, more students receiving FRL, more students from neighborhoods with lower incomes, and less adult educational attainment. The correlation with at least one of these measures of disadvantage was significant for each of the other four standards, suggesting that the issue is not limited to the new standard. However, the pervasive correlations of disadvantage measures with standard 1 may reflect the difficulties of managing human capital in these schools, which were affected more than other schools, on average, by school closings and other recent reforms.

Rubric scores are not significantly correlated with principals' responses to survey questions about their practices and their views of PPIP, except when both are correlated with student characteristics. Table 6.7 presents a correlation matrix of nine survey scales with rubric ratings for the rated principals who responded to the surveys. Of note, we find that there is no association between the principals' responses to questions about the rubric and their performance on the rubric. We do find that the scale that measures principals' ratings of the quality of school and teacher instructional improvement efforts is strongly correlated with four out of the five rubric standards. However, both this survey scale and the rubric are negatively related to the disadvantage level of the students in a school. A regression of the overall rubric rating on this scale and the demographic characteristics (not shown) indicates that the correlation is driven by the mutual relationship to affluence rather than a separate relationship between the rubric and the survey scale.

Principals' Performance on the Achievement Bonus Measures

The annual bonus of up to $10,000 is based on a set of student achievement measures. As described in Chapter Three, these measures are based primarily on achievement growth, with additional measures aimed at capturing early elementary achievement and high school progress and advanced performance.

Although achievement bonuses are pegged to absolute rather than relative targets, the bonus distribution has remained remarkably constant over time. Table 6.8 presents the distribution of bonuses that were earned based on the achievement measures in each year of the program. Although the distribution changed slightly from year to year, reflecting differences in student achievement, the median bonus was in the $2,000–4,000 interval each year. The percentage of principals earning a bonus larger than $4,000 ranged from 14 percent in year 3 to 33 percent in year 4. In general, the distribution of bonuses skewed toward lower bonuses, with approximately two-thirds of the principals earning bonuses of less than $3,000 each year. This stability suggests that an achievement bonus program can be designed so that bonuses change to reflect changes in achievement growth but do not change so much as to create the risk of an overwhelming unanticipated financial burden to the district.

Table 6.7
Correlation of Rubric Scores with Principals' Survey Responses, Year 4

Response	Rubric Average	Standard				
		1	2	3	4	5
Professional growth experiences	-0.24	-0.11	-0.03	-0.27	-0.33**	-0.25
Professional development through Leadership Academy	0.01	0.13	0.12	-0.05	-0.29	0.00
Broad support from assistant superintendent	0.12	0.11	0.13	0.10	0.05	0.06
Instructional leadership from assistant superintendent	0.24	0.23	0.26	0.15	-0.03	0.23
Time spent on instruction	0.30*	0.22	0.29	0.36**	0.08	0.16
Time spent on management	-0.01	-0.03	-0.08	0.13	-0.02	-0.01
Teachers' instructional improvement	0.61***	0.65***	0.48***	0.47***	0.18	0.42***
TLT	-0.14	-0.06	0.01	-0.15	-0.22	-0.14
Rubric	0.01	-0.02	0.07	-0.10	0.02	0.06

NOTE: * = statistically significant difference from zero ($p < 0.10$). ** = statistically significant difference from zero ($p < 0.05$). *** = statistically significant difference from zero ($p < 0.01$).

Table 6.8
Distribution of Earned Bonuses (%)

Bonus Amount ($)	Year 1 (65 principals)	Year 2 (60 principals)	Year 3 (60 principals)	Year 4 (58 principals)
0	0	0	2	2
1–2,000	11	33	40	21
2,001–4,000	65	45	45	45
4,001–6,000	18	20	10	24
6,001–8,000	6	2	2	9
8,001–10,000	0	0	2	0

Although the bonus distribution has been stable over time, there is much less stability for individual principals. As discussed in Appendix F, published separately, principals' bonus amounts varied over time not only because of variation in their performance but also because of variation in the state tests, variation in the characteristics of their students, and random measurement error. We found that only 21 percent of the total variation in the SPI-2 regular values over time and among principals can be attributed to a time-invariant value associated with each principal. This implies that, of principals who are ranked in the top quintile (i.e., the top 20 percent) of principals in a given year, approximately 29 percent will be in the top quintile in the following year. Approximately 23 percent, 20 percent, 17 percent, and 13 percent will be in the second, third, fourth, and fifth quintiles, respectively. This lack of stability for individual principals over time could reflect instability in the measure—for example, due to variation in test scaling from year to year or actual changes in principal performance from year to year.

The correlations of the achievement measures with student characteristics have not shown an advantage for any particular characteristic. As shown in Table 6.9, although the achievement measures have been significantly correlated with specific student characteristics in various years, these correlations change from year to year. This lack of persistence in correlation suggests that, as desired, the achievement measures do not show preference for principals of schools serving students with particular background characteristics.

The correlations for the achievement growth measure with student characteristics vary quite a bit from year to year. Achievement growth is based on scaled score gains, which are sensitive to changes in the state test from year to year. It is possible that these changes in the state test that favor students with certain characteristics over others lead to swings in the correlation from year to year and result in significant correlations of varying signs. Correlations also are affected by the actions that principals and teachers take to improve performance in their schools, and differences in these actions from one year to the next could alter the correlations. For example, a small number of low-income schools might make particularly large strides in achievement in a given year,

Table 6.9
Correlations Between Scores on the Achievement Bonus Measures and School Characteristics

Year	Measure	Percentage Gifted	Percentage with IEP[a]	Percentage with LEP	Percentage New to PPS[b]	Percentage Who Switched PPS Schools[c]	Percentage African American	Percentage Receiving FRL	Income[d]	Adult Education[e]
1	Achievement growth	0.32**	−0.43***	0.22	−0.14	−0.23	0.31**	−0.05	−0.21	0.15
	Third-grade reading	0.01	−0.17	0.19	−0.15	0.10	−0.12	−0.02	0.11	−0.08
	High school measures	0.17	−0.10	−0.28	0.11	0.24	0.24	0.20	−0.12	−0.07
2	Achievement growth	0.12	−0.15	−0.25	−0.47***	−0.24	0.31*	0.05	−0.07	−0.13
	Third-grade reading	0.22	−0.22	−0.04	−0.02	−0.09	−0.04	−0.18	−0.29	0.39*
	High school measures	0.41	−0.28	0.56	0.16	0.04	−0.61*	−0.59*	−0.56	0.60*
3	Achievement growth	0.21	−0.26**	0.30**	−0.11	−0.10	−0.14	−0.11	0.27**	0.32**
	Third-grade reading	0.05	−0.17	−0.12	−0.09	−0.03	−0.16	0.02	0.12	0.13
	High school measures	−0.40	0.32	−0.28	0.05	0.31	−0.09	−0.14	−0.19	−0.51*
4	Achievement growth	−0.23*	0.41***	−0.01	0.10	0.21	0.30**	0.31**	−0.34***	−0.16
	Third-grade reading	−0.03	−0.24	−0.11	−0.20	0.16	−0.12	0.03	0.02	0.02
	High school measures	−0.43	0.54	−0.13	0.35	0.29	0.46	0.51	−0.47	−0.46

NOTE: * = statistically significant difference from zero (p < 0.10). ** = statistically significant difference from zero (p < 0.05). *** = statistically significant difference from zero (p < 0.01).

[a] The existence of an IEP indicates that the student is a special-needs student (nongifted).

[b] Students who were new to PPS in year 4.

[c] Students who attended a different PPS school in year 3 than in year 4.

[d] Average income in the students' home census tracts relative to the FPL.

[e] Average adult educational attainment in the students' home census tracts.

which could influence the correlation between achievement gains and income. However, we do not have data that would help us understand why these correlations change over time.

On the other hand, the third-grade reading measure is based on a regression that controls for school characteristics and does not show these swings. The high school measures are calculated for only a very small number of schools (approximately ten), and, although the correlations with school characteristics vary quite a bit, they are rarely statistically significant.

There is little evidence that achievement growth is associated with principals' survey responses. Table 6.10 shows the correlation of nine scales formed from the principal survey responses with achievement growth and the total bonus in year 4. We find that one scale is correlated with achievement growth: The scale that measures broad support from the assistant superintendent garnered higher responses from principals who had higher achievement growth in their schools. This could suggest that assistant superintendents should support principals in ways other than just instructional leadership in order to attain higher achievement growth.

Table 6.10
Correlation of Achievement Measures with Principals' Survey Responses, Year 4

Measure	Achievement Growth	Total Bonus
Professional growth experiences	−0.08	0.05
Professional development through Leadership Academy	−0.13	−0.13
Broad support from assistant superintendent	0.29*	0.29*
Instructional leadership from assistant superintendent	0.14	0.24
Time spent on instruction	−0.06	0.02
Time spent on management	0.06	0.21
Teachers' instructional improvement	0.16	0.07
TLT	−0.12	−0.07
Rubric	−0.10	−0.02

NOTE: * = statistically significant difference from zero (p < 0.10).

There is some evidence of a positive relationship between the rubric ratings and the bonus measures. We analyzed the relationship between the achievement measures and the rubric measures using both simple correlations and multivariate techniques in all four years of the program. It is important to point out that assistant superintendents have no knowledge of principals' performance on the bonus measures for the current year when they provide their ratings. Table 6.11 presents the simple correlations between the achievement measures and the scores on each of the five standards on the

Table 6.11
Correlations Between Year 4 Achievement Bonus and Rubric Measures

Measure	Standard					
	1	2	3	4	5	Total
Achievement growth	0.24	0.26	0.26	0.31*	0.05	0.30*
PSSA math growth	0.44***	0.68***	0.39**	0.12	0.20	0.51***
PSSA reading growth	−0.06	0.08	0.00	0.19	−0.32*	−0.01
Third-grade reading	0.35*	0.02	0.14	0.21	0.14	0.23
High school measures	−0.72*	−0.42	−0.46*	0.68*	−0.27	−0.39
Total bonus amount	0.08	0.16	0.18	0.14	−0.06	0.13

NOTE: * = statistically significant difference from zero ($p < 0.10$). ** = statistically significant difference from zero ($p < 0.05$). *** = statistically significant difference from zero ($p < 0.01$).

rubric in year 4. The scores on each standard are calculated by summing the ratings (1 = rudimentary through 4 = accomplished) on each of the components for the standard, and the total score is the average for the five standards.

For the first time, we find a pattern of positive correlation between achievement growth and performance on the rubric. For math achievement growth, this positive correlation is statistically significant for the first three standards and for the total rating. The reading achievement growth measure is not positively correlated with the rubric ratings, leading to a correlation between total achievement growth and the standards that is approximately one-half that for math and only marginally significant (p-value < 0.10) for the total rating.

In earlier years, we found suggestive multivariate associations between rubric ratings and achievement growth. For example, we found that the average of the rubric ratings in years 1 and 2 was positively associated with the achievement bonus in year 2 (p-value = 0.14, N = 19). We found that the year 3 achievement bonus was positively associated with growth in the rubric from year 1 to year 2 (p-value < 0.01, N = 18). This latter analysis suggests that rubric growth has a large potential impact on the achievement bonus. For example, if a principal raised his or her performance from receiving "proficient" on all 27 components in year 1 to receiving "accomplished" on 14 components but continued receiving "proficient" on the remaining 13 in year 2, we estimate that the principal would have received $1,570 more for his or her bonus in year 3 than if his or her rubric rating had not increased. The 95-percent confidence interval on this estimate of $1,570 ranges from $510 to $2,620.

Unfortunately, the number of principals who were rated on the rubric in any particular year and especially in any particular pair of years makes most of these analyses very imprecise. Therefore, we take the collection of the findings from the four years to be suggestive of a positive relationship between the rubric ratings and the achievement measures, but our estimates are far from definitive. We recommend that the district continue to monitor the data to determine the exact nature of the relationship between the behaviors measured by the rubric and the achievement bonus.

Bonus Payments and Principals' Mobility

It is expected that the support, evaluation, and incentives associated with PPIP policies will not only help school leaders improve their performance but also change the composition of the principal workforce. The program was designed to identify the most-effective principals and provide a framework to reward them for a move to more-disadvantaged schools. The program was also designed with the expectation that principals who were not able to raise their effectiveness would be more likely to leave as they realized that their achievement measures and bonuses were at the low end of the distribution.

However, the program's ability to have an impact on the mobility of principals depends, in part, on the expectations regarding the longevity of the program. The TIF grants require that the district put forth a plan for sustainability and that the district gradually take over responsibility for incentive payments. However, principals are accustomed to frequent policy changes and might doubt that the program will be sustained. Therefore, it is an empirical question whether the program was able to have an impact on the choices of principals.

We analyzed four years of information on principals' assignments. Following each year, we observe whether each principal stays as principal at the same school, moves to become principal of a different school within the district, or leaves the role of principal in the district. For those who leave the role of principal, we observe whether they move to a role in the central office, retire, leave the district but do not retire, or move to an assistant principal role within the district. Table 6.12 describes this movement in each year of the program, as well as the average bonus for each category in the two years preceding the move. We use the two-year average bonus for two reasons. First, by averaging over two years, we gain a more precise estimate of each principal's achievement gains. Second, although the most recent year is more reflective of the principal's current activity, its data are not yet available at the time most transfer decisions are made. Therefore, we also use the prior year's bonus, which is made known to the principal in approximately October of the school year and therefore may be used to reassign principals for the following year or otherwise inform move decisions.

Mobility has remained fairly constant, and the association with average bonus, although in the expected direction, is not statistically significant. We find that the percentage of principals who have remained at their schools has stayed fairly constant throughout the program, although the percentage who have retired has declined somewhat over time. The other mobility categories do not show any particular trend over time.

Table 6.12
Principals' Mobility (%)

Year	Stay at Same School in Following Year (N = 187; average bonus $2,900)	Switch PPS Schools in Following Year (N = 19; average bonus $3,200)	Move to Central Office (N = 8; average bonus $3,300)	Retire (N = 15; average bonus $3,000)	Leave District (without retiring) (N = 8; average bonus $2,800)	Return to Assistant Principal (N = 7; average bonus $2,500)	All Principals (N = 244; average bonus $3,000)
Average over 4 years	78	7	3	6	5	3	100
1	75	5	0	11	5	5	100
2	76	11	6	5	3	0	100
3	83	5	2	5	2	5	100
4	77	9	5	3	5	2	100

NOTE: Rows may not add to 100 percent because of rounding. The average bonus shown represents the average bonus for the category in the two years preceding the move for years 2–4 and the year of the move for year 1. The differences in average achievement bonuses among the columns are not statistically significant at conventional levels.

We do not find significant differences by move type in the achievement bonuses earned preceding the moves; however, the patterns are suggestive. For example, those who moved to central office positions had higher-than-average achievement bonuses prior to their moves. Those who returned to assistant principal positions had lower-than-average achievement bonuses. This is consistent with the promotion of high-performing principals and return of low performers to positions in which they can gain more experience while being mentored. Retirees had bonuses equivalent to the overall average, as would be expected if retirement were determined by age and length of service rather than performance. Those who left the district without retiring have slightly lower achievement than the overall average, which will lead to an increase in the average performance over time.

Principals moving to higher-need schools have received above-average achievement bonuses in the past. Seven percent, or 19, principals moved to become a principal in another district school during the four years of PPIP. We examined the extent to which principals moved to schools that were more or less disadvantaged according to the district's formula for determining which schools receive the high-need premium for the achievement bonus. The principals were evenly split between moving to schools with rankings that indicate higher needs and schools with lower needs. The two-year average bonus is approximately the same for those who go to schools with higher and lower needs. However, there is a strong association between the achievement bonus amount that is known at the time of reassignment and whether a principal goes to a higher-need school. Principals who went to higher-need schools earned approximately $1,900 more in bonus in the first year of the two-year average than principals who went to low-need schools (p-value < 0.05). This is consistent with the district's intention to place higher-performing principals in higher-need schools.

Turnover is very high among principals at high-need schools. We also examined whether high- or low-need schools were more likely to experience the loss of a principal. We find that a school's high-need rank has a strong association with principal turnover. Schools in the most disadvantaged quartile had a 43-percent annual turnover rate, 23 percentage points higher than other schools (p-value < 0.001).

Summary

The performance of principals on the rubric did not vary substantially over the four years of the program, with almost all principals rated in the proficient or accomplished level on almost all standards each year. We also found that the ratings of the various standards were highly correlated and that novices had significantly lower scores than experienced principals on the rubric. Rubric scores varied across school configurations, but the relationship has changed over time. In year 4, rubric scores were correlated with student characteristics, but this was not the case in prior years. The distribution of achievement bonuses remained stable throughout the program, and the bonus measure was not correlated with student characteristics from year to year.

We also examined the relationship of achievement growth to performance on the rubric. The PPIP TOA presumes that principals who perform better as measured by the rubric will have greater achievement gains, and we did find evidence that that achievement growth was positively associated with performance on the rubric. However, this finding is somewhat tentative, and the district should continue to monitor this relationship.

Finally, we analyzed principals' mobility and its relationship to achievement growth and the level of disadvantage among students. We did not find a statistically significant relationship between the achievement bonus and particular moves, although principals moving into central office roles had higher achievement bonuses than principals returning to assistant principal roles. We found that principals switching to more-disadvantaged schools had significantly higher prior average achievement bonuses than principals switching to less disadvantaged schools.

CHAPTER SEVEN

Student Achievement Trends

The primary objective of PPIP is to improve school leadership as a means of raising student achievement across the district. In this chapter, we present findings related to student achievement and achievement gaps through year 4 of the initiative, with the goal of understanding how achievement changed throughout the course of PPIP. It is important to remember that many reforms occurred simultaneously in PPS and that changes in factors outside the district's control could also have influenced achievement trends. Therefore, caution should be used when attributing any causal impact of PPIP on achievement.

Achievement Trends

Achievement growth as measured by the SPI-2 regular (mathematics and reading combined) was positive in every year of PPIP implementation. Table 7.1 presents the average growth percentage on these measures from two years before PPIP was instituted through year 4 of the initiative. These figures reflect the average of the figures for each school. Therefore, schools with fewer students included in the calculation will be given more weight than they would if the average were calculated directly from student-level data.

There was a considerable dip in achievement growth one year prior to the beginning of PPIP. Approximately one-quarter of the district's schools that served grades K–8 were closed, leading to the relocation of many students for this school year. We expect that this disruption is responsible for much of the achievement dip in this year. Achievement growth in the first year of PPIP rebounded to approximately the level that had existed before the school closings.

This was followed by three years of declining growth. In the fourth year of the initiative, the district experienced the highest growth of any year for which data are available. Achievement growth in mathematics was particularly high, although growth in reading was higher than in any but one year.

Table 7.1
Achievement Trends as Measured by the School Performance Index 2: Average Percentage Achievement Growth District-Wide

Measure	Two Years Prior	One Year Prior	Year 1	Year 2	Year 3	Year 4
SPI-2 regular (combined)	3.22	0.94	3.36	3.11	2.36	4.12
SPI-2 regular (math)	3.13	0.21	3.68	2.35	2.12	4.44
SPI-2 regular (reading)	3.31	1.67	3.03	3.86	2.60	3.79
SPI-2 third-grade reading	—	1.79	2.44	0.10	−0.01	−0.15

NOTE: SPI-2 regular measures are the student-weighted average percentage growth for all qualifying students in grades 4 through 8. A value of 10 percent earned a full bonus. SPI-2 regular calculation excludes high school students because of changes over time to the high school test portfolio. SPI-2 third-grade reading emphasis is the average percentage difference from third-grade reading PSSA scores of PPS students with similar characteristics during the previous two years. A value of 10 percent earned a full bonus. The SPI-2 third-grade reading emphasis measure cannot be calculated for 2005–2006 because the third-grade PSSA was not available for two prior years.

On the other hand, the average SPI-2 third-grade reading emphasis measure continued its decline to below zero, although the average values for years 2, 3, and 4 are very similar.

The SPI-2 has several limitations for measuring achievement growth. Some, such as its reliance on students who were enrolled in PPS for two consecutive years, cannot be eliminated because these are the only students for whom we can calculate achievement growth. In fact, declining enrollment throughout the period and associated changes in student demographics might be confounding factors that contribute to the observed trends. Other limitations can be addressed by calculating additional measures. We address some of these in the following sections.

The patterns over time in achievement growth are not sensitive to several key design choices that were used in the SPI-2 formula. One limitation that can be addressed is that the SPI-2 includes only those students who are in the same school at the beginning and the end of the year. This design feature was adopted in order to focus on the students for whom a specific principal is likely to have the largest impact. However, it is important to monitor the achievement growth of as many district students as possible. Furthermore, the difference in achievement growth between transient students and the students included in the SPI-2 is not known. In general, transient students have lower achievement growth than other students. Furthermore, because transient students do not count toward the PPIP bonus, they may have had less programming directed toward them after the inception of PPIP. However, the emphasis of the bonus system on students who have lower prior scores might lead principals to implement programming that works to the benefit of these students, and their achievement growth might have improved more during PPIP than that of other students.

As shown in the top panel of Table 7.2, in most years, the achievement growth of all continuing students is slightly lower than those for students who were in a single school the entire year. It is not surprising that achievement growth would be lower for students who change schools during the year. The difference between growth of all continuing students and that of students who did not change schools during the year is approximately the same before and after the initiation of PPIP. This suggests that the PPIP bonus formula based only on students who did not change schools during the year did not lead school staff to neglect students who were not counted in the SPI-2.

Another difference between Table 7.1 and the top panel of Table 7.2 is that Table 7.1 presents the average over the schools whereas Table 7.2 presents the average over students. Middle schools tend to be larger and have more students per grade, so Table 7.1 underrepresents middle school students. For example, in year 4, reading achievement grew more and mathematics achievement grew less for middle school students than for elementary grade students, leading to a reversal in the size of growth estimates in the two tables.

Another continuing concern regarding the SPI-2 is that it is based on the PSSA scale, which is designed to be constant over time. The district designed the SPI-2 this way to maximize transparency. It was thought that any further transformations or scaling would cause the SPI-2 to be less easily understood and less accepted by the

Table 7.2
Achievement Growth With and Without Scaling, by State Performance: Average Percentage Growth of All Students with Prior-Year Pennsylvania System of School Assessment Scores

Measure	Two Years Before	One Year Before	Year 1	Year 2	Year 3	Year 4
Using PSSA scale						
Combined math and reading	3.25	0.90	3.33	3.05	2.26	3.72
Math	3.10	0.08	3.73	2.33	2.01	3.18
Reading	3.39	1.73	2.93	3.76	2.51	4.26
Relative to state performance						
Combined math and reading	1.98	−0.61	0.62	0.79	−0.03	1.56
Math	2.46	−0.90	0.98	0.29	−0.75	1.53
Reading	1.49	−0.33	0.26	1.30	0.68	1.58

NOTE: The top three rows use the SPI-2 regular formula of calculating each student's score in the current and previous years and dividing by the previous year's score before averaging. The bottom three rows first take each student's score and subtract the state average and divide by the state standard deviation for that subject, grade, and year. This number is then multiplied by 220, the typical standard deviation, and added to 1,400, the intended mean of the PSSA. This standardized score is then plugged into the SPI-2 regular formula described above.

principals. However, given the difficulties of designing tests year after year that have exactly equivalent scales, there is the possibility that some of the observed variation over time is due to variation in the difficulty of the test rather than variation in underlying achievement growth. This would be especially problematic if this variation in difficulty from year to year affected some grades more than others because it could put principals of some types of schools at a disadvantage. To address this possible variation, we rescaled the scores using a reference group. In the bottom panel of Table 7.2, we present achievement growth for all continuing students, after rescaling by the state's mean and standard deviation in each subject in each grade in each year.

The achievement growth rates relative to the state show a similar pattern to the unadjusted growth rates, although at a lower level of growth. This suggests that the use of the more transparent PSSA measure has not masked the variation in achievement growth.

Achievement growth estimated from a low-stakes early elementary reading test yields similar values to the SPI-2 measures. Another limitation of the SPI-2 is that it does not use an actual growth measure for grades K–3 but instead uses a third-grade reading emphasis measure based on the comparison of third-grade reading PSSA scores in the current year with those of similar students district-wide in the previous two years. This comparison measure was adopted by the district after ruling out the use of an existing early elementary diagnostic test, DIBELS, for high-stakes purposes and ruling out the addition of a new early elementary summative assessment. The comparison measure is intended to capture the ability of the principal and school to improve achievement during the early elementary years. However, by using information on only third graders, it is necessarily inferior to a true growth measure that is based on a change in assessment scores for students in all early elementary grades.

Although DIBELS is not appropriate for high-stakes decisions, in part because it is implemented through direct interaction of the school staff with the students, it can be used to measure reading achievement growth of K–3 students in each year. We have calculated achievement growth rates using the spring administration of DIBELS in grades K–3 and the fall kindergarten administration of DIBELS.

We do this for two reasons. First, we would like to compare achievement growth using this measure with the third-grade reading emphasis comparison measure. DIBELS does not claim to measure exactly the same skills as the PSSA reading test. At the third-grade level, the only DIBELS test given in the spring of the third grade is the oral reading fluency test. The scores on this test have a correlation with the third-grade PSSA reading test of 0.67, indicating that students who have a high score on one test are likely to have a high score on the other. Therefore, we construct a DIBELS growth measure and use it to address the following questions: (1) Do the school-level DIBELS growth measures have a high correlation with third-grade reading emphasis measures in a given year? (2) Do the district-wide trends over time in the DIBELS measure resemble those of the comparison measure?

Second, we would like to compare the achievement growth for K–3 students with that already calculated for grades 4–8. One criticism of any incentive program is that "you get what you pay for." Has achievement growth in the early elementary grades lagged that of grades 4–8 because it was not rewarded as directly?

Using DIBELS has the added benefit that it uses the same test repeatedly at each level. Therefore, the issue of whether scales are comparable from year to year that has arisen with the PSSA is not a concern.

In some grades, multiple DIBELS tests are given. Therefore, we take the principal factor of all the tests reported for those grades. The principal factor is a weighted combination of the tests that captures the variation that the tests have in common for the sample of students in each grade with multiple tests. In order to create a growth scale that is similar to that based on the PSSA, we take the single score or principal factor at each grade level (kindergarten in the fall and K–3 in the spring), pooled for 2004–2005 through 2008–2009, and set the mean and standard deviation of this entire sample to be the same as that of the third-grade PSSA during the same period. These standardized scores are then turned into a percentage growth measure in the same manner as PSSA scores for SPI-2. DIBELS scores are not available except for kindergarten and third grade after 2008–2009, making it no longer possible to calculate a DIBELS-based achievement growth measure.

Table 7.3 presents the correlation of the school-level DIBELS achievement growth measure with the third-grade reading measure for the years for which we have both measures.

The DIBELS measure is positively correlated with the SPI-2 third-grade reading emphasis measure in two of the three years, but none of the correlations is statistically significant at conventional levels. This suggests that the third-grade reading emphasis

Table 7.3
Correlation of School Performance Index 2 Third-Grade Reading Emphasis and Percentage Growth in the Dynamic Indicators of Basic Early Literacy Skills

One Year Before	Year 1[a]	Year 2
0.21	0.01	0.19

NOTE: SPI-2 third-grade reading emphasis is the average percentage difference from third-grade reading PSSA scores of PPS students with similar characteristics during the previous two years. Percentage growth DIBELS is the average percentage growth of the primary factor of DIBELS scores in K–3, standardized to a PSSA scale. DIBELS scores are not available for grades 1 and 2 in year 3 or for kindergarten entry or grade 2 in year 4, which prevents extending this table beyond year 2.

[a] Year 1 DIBELS growth is for only K–2 because third-grade spring DIBELS data are incomplete.

measure is, at best, rewarding only some of the principals that achieve the greatest achievement growth, at least as measured by DIBELS.

Table 7.4 adds the achievement growth as measured by DIBELS to the trends presented in Tables 7.1 and 7.2 so that we can examine its trends in comparison with that of other achievement measures.

As with the other achievement growth measures, the DIBELS measure shows a dramatic dip in the year prior to PPIP, a rebound in the following year, and then a decline. As would be expected from a low-stakes test with a constant scale, it shows less growth than the high-stakes SPI-2 regular growth measure and more growth than when we measure relative to statewide growth. It shows less growth than the third-grade reading comparison measure in the first two years for which we have both measures and more growth in the third. Along with the low correlations with the third-grade reading comparison measure, this provides evidence that the two are, at best, imperfectly related.

Table 7.4
Comparing Dynamic Indicators of Basic Early Literacy Skills Kindergarten Through Third-Grade Achievement Trends and Bonus Achievement Measures: Average Percentage Growth over Students with Prior-Year Scores

Measure	Two Years Prior	One Year Prior	Year 1	Year 2	Year 3
SPI-2 regular (combined)	3.22	0.94	3.36	3.11	2.36
SPI-2 regular (math)	3.13	0.21	3.68	2.35	2.12
SPI-2 regular (reading)	3.31	1.67	3.03	3.86	2.60
SPI-2 third-grade reading emphasis	—	1.79	2.44	0.10	−0.01
Relative to state performance					
Combined math and reading	1.98	−0.61	0.62	0.79	−0.03
Math	2.46	−0.90	0.98	0.29	−0.75
Reading	1.49	−0.33	0.26	1.30	0.68
DIBELS achievement growth	1.70	0.19	1.27	0.94	—

NOTE: SPI-2 regular measures are the student-weighted average percentage growth for all qualifying students in grades 4–8. A value of 10 percent earned a full bonus. The SPI-2 regular calculation excludes high school students because of changes over time to the high school test portfolio. SPI-2 third-grade reading emphasis is the average percentage difference from third-grade reading PSSA scores of PPS students with similar characteristics during the previous two years. A value of 10 percent earned a full bonus. The SPI-2 third-grade reading emphasis measure cannot be calculated for the second year prior to PPIP (2005–06) because the third-grade PSSA was not available for two prior years. DIBELS scores are not available for year 3. DIBELS achievement growth is the average percentage growth of the primary factor of DIBELS scores in K–3, standardized to a PSSA scale. Year 1 DIBELS growth is only K–2 because third-grade spring DIBELS data are incomplete.

In sum, student achievement growth in PPS has surpassed the growth experienced by students in the rest of the state in three out of the four years since the beginning of PPIP. PPS student achievement growth in year 4 was at its highest level since the advent of testing in consecutive grades has enabled growth calculations. The evidence is mixed regarding achievement growth among students not included in the achievement growth component of the bonus formula. Early elementary achievement as measured by the third-grade reading comparison leveled off in years 3 and 4. Growth among transient students is lower than growth among students included in the bonus formula, but this difference has not changed since the initiation of PPIP.

Addressing Racial/Ethnic and Socioeconomic Achievement Gaps

Closing race and poverty gaps is a stated goal of PPIP. In this section, we examine the trends in these gaps from before the initiation of PPIP through the present, using several definitions of the gap. Next, we examine the evidence regarding the impact of specific mechanisms by which PIPP is expected to reduce these gaps.

It is necessary to examine achievement gaps using scale scores for continuing students rather than proficiency rates for all students in order to measure actual growth throughout the range of achievement. Gaps and changes in gaps can be measured in many ways. AYP and state policy have led to a focus on proficiency levels, and the district has reported the proficiency gap and how it has changed over time for successive cohorts of students. Proficiency is a useful and policy-relevant metric, and the goal of supporting successive cohorts of minority and low-income students to perform better than their predecessors is also important, but using proficiency as the sole measure of success misses two key issues: (1) reliance on gaps in percentage proficient measures changes at only one point of the achievement distribution, and (2) use of successive cohorts confounds changes in the composition of the district with changes in the performance over time of the students who remained in the district during that time frame. Therefore, we prefer to report changes in the achievement gap measured using average scale scores for students who took the PSSA in two successive years.[1]

Analysis using continuing students captures the achievement growth of individuals who were educated during the year, rather than differences among groups entering and leaving the tested population. To demonstrate the importance of using the performance from continuing students rather than comparing cohorts, Figure 7.1 shows the percentage proficient or advanced in the 2006–2007 and 2007–2008 school years for various groups of African American students and non–African American students. (We adopt the convention of dividing the PPS student population into African

---

[1] See Center on Education Policy, 2007, for a more detailed explanation of the advantages of this approach to measuring gaps.

Figure 7.1
Change in Achievement Gap Measured by Percentage Proficient or Advanced

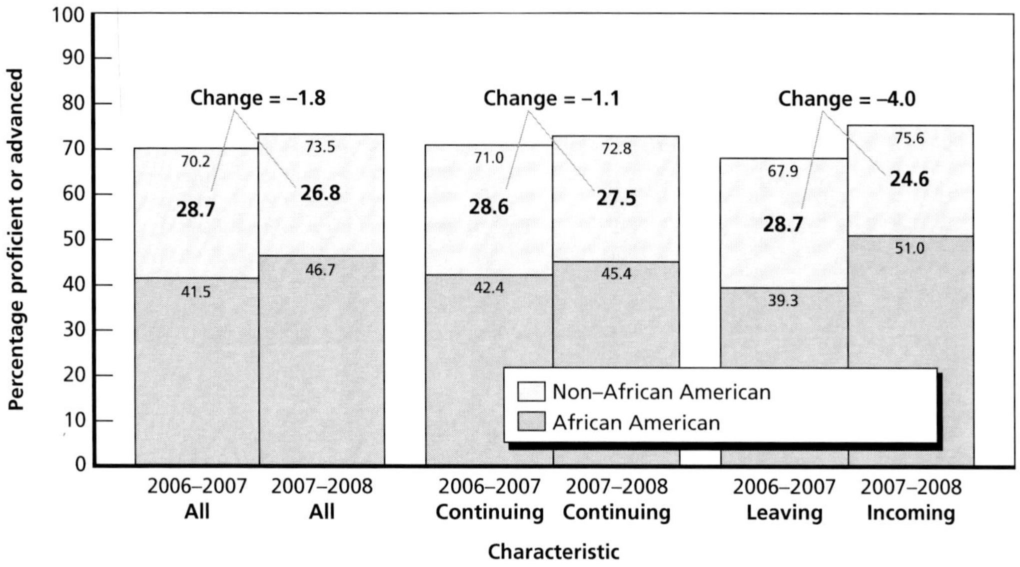

American and non–African American students. This categorization reflects the status of African Americans as Pittsburgh's only sizable disadvantaged minority.) The set of bars on the left of the figure is for all students in grades 3–8 in each of the years. The achievement gap shrinks by 1.8 percentage points from 28.7 percent to 26.8 percent.

However, the 2006–2007 group of students contains some who continue to take the PSSA in PPS in the following year and some who do not. Likewise, the 2007–2008 group of students contains some who continued from the previous year and some who were new to PSSA testing in PPS. Because the group of students who continue from 2006–2007 to 2007–2008 consists of the same students in both 2006–2007 and 2007–2008, the change in their performance reflects an increase in the achievement for the members of that group who moved from below proficient to proficient or above. The difference in the proficiency rates between the 2006–2007 group leaving the tested group of students and the 2007–2008 group entering the group of tested students reflects many things, but it does not reflect a contribution of PPS to achievement. Most of the students who leave the tested group do so either because they move from eighth to ninth grade or because they leave PPS to go to school somewhere else. The students who leave include about one-third of the tested students each year. Most of the entering students are either entering third grade or coming to PPS from other school systems. Likewise, they are about one-third of the students. Therefore, as we compare a given year's performance with the prior year's performance, as is done in the two bars at the left of Figure 7.1, only two-thirds of the included scores are for students who actually took the test in both years.

If we focus on the students who are in the district in both years—in this case, 2006–2007 and 2007–2008, we see from the two bars in the middle of Figure 7.1 that the gap in the percentage proficient between African American students and non–African American students decreased by 1.1 percent rather than the 1.8 percent calculated for the change between the two cohorts. Looking at the pair of bars at the right of the figure, we see that this is because the achievement gap for the incoming group of students is much smaller (24.6 percent) than for any of the other groups of students.

The other difficulty with focusing on the bars in Figure 7.1 is that they reflect only whether students are on one side or another of the proficiency cutoff rather than reflecting the performance of students throughout the achievement range. Test-score gains that move students from below basic to basic or from proficient to advanced, as well as gains that occur within one of those categories, are not captured using the percentage-proficient metric. The TIF steering committee explicitly chose an achievement bonus measure based on PSSA scale scores rather than one based on achievement levels in order to account for achievement growth at all places in the achievement range.

There is another reason to prefer a measure based on scale scores rather than achievement levels when comparing two groups with very different average achievement. The group that experiences the largest gains in percentage scoring above proficient is not always the group with the largest average scale score gain. Figure 7.2 demonstrates this using the data from the set of students who took the PSSA in both 2006–2007 and 2007–2008. This is the same group that is represented in the middle pair of bars in Figure 7.1.

The top panel of Figure 7.2 shows the familiar bell curve, also known as the normal distribution, which is a way to represent the scores for African American students who took the PSSA in both 2006–2007 and 2007–2008. The percentage of these students who were proficient or above rose from 42.4 percent in 2006–2007 to 45.4 percent in 2007–2008, an increase of 3 percentage points. The average scale score of all these students improved from 1,227 to 1,259, for an improvement of 32 points. One way to think about the relationship between these two improvements is to imagine what would happen if every African American student improved his or her score by 32 points. Not only would the average increase by 32 points, but the entire bell curve would shift to the right by 32 points, moving some students who were just below the proficiency cutoff to just above. These students are represented by the shaded area of the 2007–2008 bell curve. Notice that the percentage of students who become proficient is affected not only by the distance of the shift but also by the number of students on the cusp of proficiency, which is related to the height of the curve at the cutoff.

The bottom panel of Figure 7.2 presents the same information for non–African American students. As was shown in the middle bars of Figure 7.1, that group of students increased from 71.0 percent proficient or above to 72.8 percent, for a gain of

Figure 7.2
Measurement of Changes in the Achievement Gap

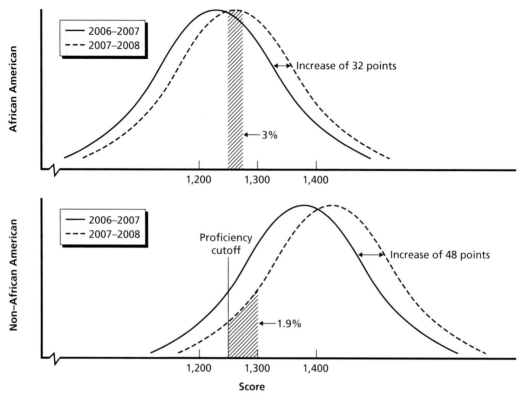

1.9 percentage points. Therefore, the achievement gap as measured by proficiency rates decreased by 1.1 percentage points. However, the average scale score of those students increased by 48 points, which is 16 more than that of the African American students. Therefore, when we use a measure that reflects growth throughout the achievement distribution, we see that the achievement gap actually increased between 2006–2007 and 2007–2008. Figure 7.2 shows that fewer non–African American students are on the cusp of proficiency than African American students, which accounts for a smaller percentage moving across the proficiency threshold even though the average increase in scale scores was larger.

Figure 7.3 repeats Figure 7.1, showing the importance of using the scores for continuing students, only this time average scale score is used rather than the percentage proficient or above. Once again, we see that the difference between the cohort comparison and the change in the gap for continuing students is largely due to the small achievement gap for incoming students, which is due to unusually low average scores for the incoming non–African American students.

Figure 7.3
Change in Achievement Gap Measured by Average Scale Score

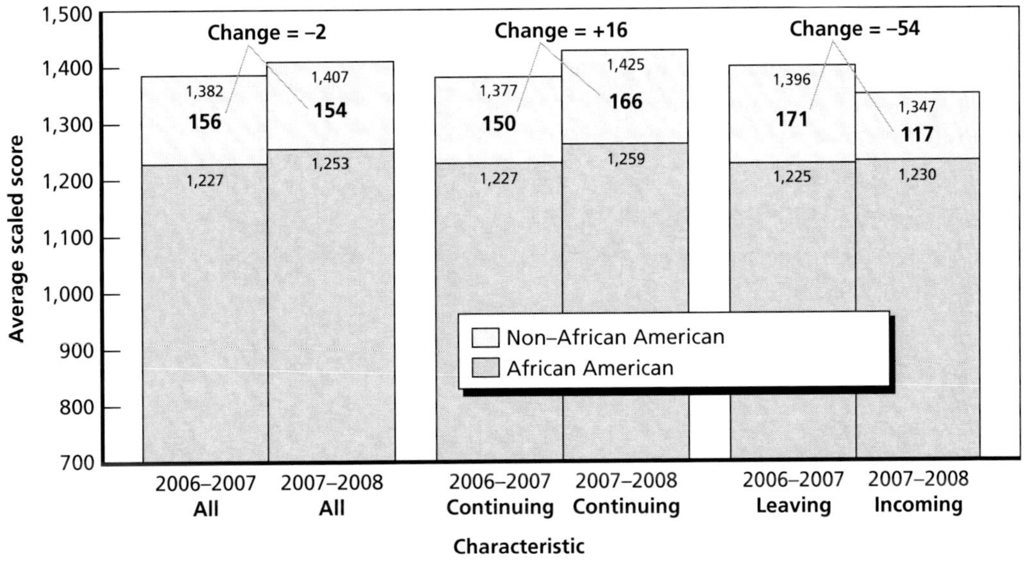

RAND MG1223-7.3

When measured using scale scores for continuing students, race and poverty gaps have been increasing every year since before PPIP. We turn now to an examination of the change in the race and poverty achievement gaps since prior to the beginning of PPIP. Table 7.5 presents the change in the race achievement gap measured four ways each year. The first two sets of three rows use the percentage proficient or above for all students and for continuing students. The second two sets of three rows use the average scale score for all and for continuing students. As we have demonstrated, only the last three rows accurately capture the change in average performance for a well-defined group of students.

Table 7.5 shows that, in the four years since the beginning of PPIP, the achievement gap has increased every year when measured by the average achievement gain of continuing students, even though it has decreased in most years according to the other measures. These other measures reflect the relatively large number of African American students near the proficiency cutoff, the changing composition of the tested students, or both. It is worth noting, however, that the increases in the achievement gap of 5 to 7 percent in years 2, 3, and 4 are smaller than the increases were in the two prior years.

Table 7.6 provides the same information for students grouped by poverty status rather than by race. Poverty status is determined by whether a student receives FRL. The same issues of using a well-defined group of students and using scores throughout the range of achievement pertain to this analysis as well. However, because the number of students not receiving FRL near the proficiency cutoff is larger than that for non–

Table 7.5
Change in Race Achievement Gap Before and After the Pittsburgh Principal Incentive Program Was Initiated

Measure	Two Years Prior	One Year Prior	Year 1	Year 2	Year 3	Year 4
Change in percentage proficient						
All students						
Non–African American students, change in percentage proficient	1.5	−0.9	3.3	1.0	0.2	2.4
African American students, change in percentage proficient	3.5	−1.4	5.2	2.4	0.8	3.9
Change in achievement gap	−2.0	0.5	−1.8	−1.4	−0.5	−1.5
Continuing students						
Non–African American students, change in percentage proficient	1.6	−1.7	1.9	1.1	−0.9	2.2
African American students, change in percentage proficient	2.5	−3.2	3.0	2.1	0.4	3.1
Change in achievement gap	−0.9	1.5	−1.1	−1.0	−1.2	−0.9
Change in scale score						
All students						
Non–African American students, change in average score	29	−9	25	7	4	14
African American students, change in average score	26	−3	26	15	3	18
Change in achievement gap	3	−6	−1	−8	1	−4
Continuing students						
Non–African American students, change in average score	36	11	48	37	28	42
African American students, change in average score	29	0	32	32	22	37
Change in achievement gap	7	11	15	5	7	5

African American students, the impact on the calculation of using average score rather than proficiency rate is less dramatic. In fact, the measure using proficiency rates for all students indicates an increase in the poverty achievement gap in all years except year 4, as does the preferred measure that uses the average scale score.

In sum, we conclude that, contrary to the goal of PPIP, when we examine the change in scale score for continuing students, the race and poverty achievement gaps have been increasing since the beginning of PPIP. In every year, the change in the gap

Table 7.6
Change in Poverty Achievement Gap Before and After the Pittsburgh Principal Incentive Program Was Initiated

Measure	Two Years Prior	One Year Prior	Year 1	Year 2	Year 3	Year 4
Change in percentage proficient						
All students						
Students not receiving FRL, change in percentage proficient	5.8	0.9	6.6	4.7	4.4	2.9
Students receiving FRL, change in percentage proficient	2.9	−1.5	4.8	2.3	0.4	3.6
Change in achievement gap	2.9	2.4	1.8	2.4	4.0	−0.7
Continuing students						
Students not receiving FRL, change in percentage proficient	1.4	−2.0	2.3	1.3	−0.8	2.4
Students receiving FRL, change in percentage proficient	2.7	−2.9	2.6	1.8	0.0	2.9
Change in achievement gap	−1.3	1.0	−0.4	−0.6	−0.8	−0.5
Change in scale score						
All students						
Students not receiving FRL, change in average score	45	5	46	31	31	14
Students receiving FRL, change in average score	33	−4	24	15	3	18
Change in achievement gap	12	9	22	16	28	−4
Continuing students						
Students not receiving FRL, change in average score	34	8	49	39	38	44
Students receiving FRL, change in average score	31	3	33	32	20	37
Change in achievement gap	3	5	17	7	18	7

is positive, meaning that the more advantaged group is experiencing more achievement growth than the less advantaged group. The rate of increase of the poverty gap appears to have increased since the beginning of PPIP as well. In every year since the beginning of PPIP, the growth in the gap has been larger than it was in the years immediately prior to PPIP.

We cannot attribute this increase in race and poverty achievement gaps directly to PPIP. Many other factors are affecting achievement growth in the district. It could be the case that PPIP is having the desired effect on the achievement gap but other factors more than offset this effect. PPIP aims to improve achievement of all students through a combination of professional development, evaluation, and incentives. Any of these efforts might have an impact on the achievement gap, if they were to raise the scores by poor or African American students by a different amount than nonpoor or non–African American students.

However, there are two specific ways in which the design of the achievement bonus program is intended to reduce the achievement gaps. First, by rewarding average percentage growth rather than average growth, the bonus formula rewards every point of achievement growth by previously low-achieving students more than every point of growth by previously high-achieving students. Second, starting in year 3, PPS designated some schools as high-need schools and rewards achievement growth more in those schools. We examine whether there is evidence that these larger incentives are leading to greater growth by the targeted students.

In year 4, achievement growth for previously low-scoring students has accelerated, which is consistent with a design feature of the bonus formula and may reduce achievement gaps in the future. One way to assess whether principals may be responding to the financial incentives available from growing the scores of their lowest-scoring students is to examine a curve that represents the average percentage change in scale score at each value of the previous year's score. If principals are responding to the incentives by increasing practices that lead to score growth by the lowest-scoring students, we should see a greater increase in score growth for these students now than we saw prior to the implementation of the bonus program. This would, in turn, likely reduce the achievement gaps because poor and African American students are overrepresented among low-achieving students.

We have estimated the average percentage growth by students at all levels of prior achievement for the past four years. These estimates only use within-school variation in previous achievement and achievement growth, thereby focusing on whether, within each school, students who previously scored poorly on the PSSA have increased their scores by more than students who previously scored well. We would expect this to always be the case because of regression to the mean. On average, the previously low-scoring students are more likely to have scored below their own norm (i.e., "had a bad day") than previously high-scoring students, so we are not surprised to find that previously low-scoring students always have greater score growth on average than previously high-scoring students. However, our hypothesis is that initiation of PPIP will make this difference even more pronounced because principals are now given a financial incentive to direct more resources toward low-scoring students.

Figure 7.4 shows the estimated curves for one year prior to PPIP and four years following initial implementation. The expected response to the incentives would be reflected by curves that increase more for lower-scoring students than for higher-scoring students—that is, curves that become higher and steeper as the years pass. We see

Figure 7.4
Average Percentage Growth in the Pennsylvania System of School Assessment Scale Score (math and reading averaged)

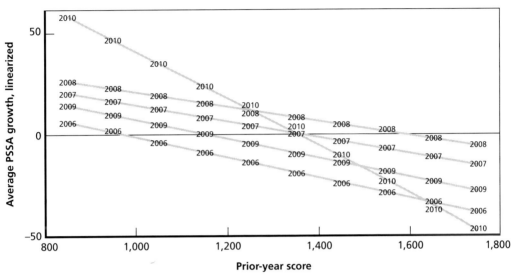

RAND *MG1223-7.4*

that the curves are higher in the first three years after the incentive program began than they were in year 1 (2006–2007). We also see that the curve in year 4 (2010–2011) is steeper than in any of the previous years. This recent curve suggests that the lowest-scoring students are attaining greater growth than high-scoring students than they were previously. This development could have a positive effect on the poverty and race gaps in math achievement, even though it has not been sufficient to offset other factors that have increased these gaps.

Achievement growth in high-need schools increased in the second year of the high-need bonus premium. As described in Chapter Six, PPS designated approximately one-quarter of its schools as high-need schools in years 3 and 4. The achievement bonus was amended to provide a premium for achievement growth to principals of these schools. Economic theory would predict that this incentive would lead to greater achievement growth in these schools because the return is higher. Of course, it could be that these schools have low achievement growth because their students face many disadvantages. Therefore, we again look at the difference between achievement growth since the initiation of this premium for schools that received the high-need designation and achievement growth in these same schools prior to the availability of the premium.

The four schools with the largest high-need premium received double bonus dollars for each percentage point of achievement growth, with prorated premiums for the other 12 or 13 schools in each year. We compared the achievement growth in these schools following their designation as high-need schools and the growth they experienced prior to the amendment of the program and to the growth of schools receiving the regular bonus.

In year 3, we found only modest evidence that the high-need premium was leading to increased growth (p-value = 0.20). However, in year 4, the four schools with double bonus dollars experienced 1.5 percentage points more growth than expected, and the other schools, receiving smaller high-need premiums, also have proportionately higher growth than expected (p-value < 0.01). Finding this, we conclude that, by year 4, the high-need premium appears to be accelerating growth in the most-disadvantaged schools. This should also work to reduce the race and poverty achievement gaps as years pass.

Summary

The analyses described in this chapter show that achievement growth was positive during PPIP for most measures of achievement, with the exception of the SPI-2 third-grade reading emphasis measure. In the final year of our evaluation, achievement growth in grades 4–8 in both math and reading rose to their highest levels since the data permitted calculation of these measures. By this measure, achievement growth accelerated since the beginning of PPIP, consistent with the district's goal of promoting more-effective school leadership as a means of improving student achievement.

Race and poverty achievement gaps increased throughout the time of PPIP, when measured by average growth throughout the range of achievement for students who take the PSSA test in consecutive years, which is not consistent with the goal of the program. However, we found evidence in year 4 that the percentage growth aspect of the design bonus, which differentially rewarded growth by low-achieving students, could be offsetting other pressures that raise the achievement gaps. Furthermore, we found evidence that the high-need premium that was instituted in year 3 has had a beneficial impact on the achievement gaps.

CHAPTER EIGHT

Key Findings and Recommendations

Although it is not possible to determine with certainty the extent to which PPIP achieved the district's objectives in terms of its effects on teaching and learning, the evaluation did produce several findings that can help us understand how the reform worked in PPS, and that can inform other efforts to develop and adopt new principal evaluation and compensation systems. In this chapter, we summarize the main findings from the evaluation, which are organized according to the research questions listed in Chapter One. We then provide recommendations to guide the development and implementation of similar reforms.

Key Findings

What Is the District's Theory of Action Regarding How the Pittsburgh Principal Incentive Program Is Expected to Promote Improved Student Outcomes?

PPIP used a combination of capacity-building interventions, including incentives, to change principals' instructional leadership practices in ways that were intended to improve instruction and, ultimately, student learning. The data that we gathered from district staff and documentation informed the development of a TOA that was vetted with district staff and that illustrates the mechanisms through which PPIP is expected to achieve the desired outcomes. PPIP includes three categories of *capacity-building interventions*: professional development, evaluation and feedback, and incentives. It is noteworthy that, although many current policy discussions regarding teacher and principal evaluation focus on the monetary incentives, these were just one aspect of PPIP, and district staff emphasized that they did not view the incentives as the most important aspect of the program. Instead, district-level staff viewed the support and feedback interventions as having the most potential impact on principal performance. Principals themselves were much more likely to attribute changes in their leadership behavior to support and feedback than to financial incentives. The capacity-building interventions, particularly the rubric-based feedback provided as part of the evaluation process, were intended to improve student achievement through their direct *impact on principals*, with this impact expected to take place through three mechanisms: selecting and developing the pool of principals, enhancing the knowledge and skills of principals, and refocusing principals' leadership practices to emphasize activities that are likely to improve student achievement. These effects on principals were hypothesized to lead to an *impact on schools* and then an *impact on classrooms*, with the latter focused on improving the quality of instruction. The ultimate goal is an *impact on students* manifested by improved achievement. Importantly, the district implemented PPIP in a broader context of multiple reforms that were also focused on improving teaching and learning, and information gathered from district and school staff suggests that the various reforms were perceived as working well together and pointing toward a common goal. Articulating the TOA in this way could be helpful for states or districts that are developing their own systems and for communicating to school staff and to the public how the reform is expected to work (and, in particular, that it is not all about the monetary rewards).

How Were the Pittsburgh Principal Incentive Program Capacity-Building Interventions Implemented, and How Have Principals Responded to Them?

Most principals reported that the capacity-building interventions helped them improve their leadership practices. Overall, principals rated their PPIP-supported professional development experiences highly, and majorities of principals responded that nearly all forms of professional development contributed to their professional growth. This finding has been fairly consistent throughout the three years of survey data collection but with small changes in the ratings of specific types of professional development. In particular, in year 4, majorities of principals reported that learning walks with their internal instructional leadership team and participation in their own DPG projects contributed to their professional growth. The district has emphasized professional development to support principals in their roles as coaches and evaluators of teachers, and Leadership Academy professional development has served as a key mechanism for delivering this support. Most principals agreed that professional development delivered through the PPIP Leadership Academy helped them improve their skills across multiple leadership domains, most strongly in the areas of monitoring teachers' instruction and providing feedback to teachers. In addition, nearly two-thirds of principals reported that one-on-one coaching from their assistant superintendents made a moderate or large contribution to their professional growth.

   Principals viewed the rubric as helpful and realistic but expressed concerns about fairness and consistency of ratings across assistant superintendents. Large majorities of principals indicated that the rubric-based evaluation process helped them think about their leadership strengths and weaknesses, and almost no principals reported negative effects on their relationships with their assistant superintendents. In addition, in year 4, only 16 percent of principals endorsed the notion that it would be difficult for them to earn a salary increment because of conditions in the school that prevent the principal from engaging in the desired practices. The changes that the district made to the rubric and evaluation process over the course of PPIP implementation, particularly the reduction in the number of standards and the increased focus on principals' roles as instructional leaders and managers of human capital, were well received by principals. In particular, principals reported that the new rubric standards were well aligned with the work they were doing to support and evaluate teachers. At the same time, majorities of principals expressed concerns about fairness throughout the course of the evaluation, including a perception that different assistant superintendents used different criteria for assigning ratings and a lack of confidence that the rubric did a good job distinguishing effective from ineffective principals or was fair to all principals regardless of the type of school in which they worked.

Principals' opinions about the bonus measure were mixed, but large majorities expressed skepticism about its validity. Most principals did not report negative effects of the bonus on principal morale or on principals' willingness to collaborate, and fewer than half agreed that "[r]ewarding individual principals based on test score gains is problematic because the principal has limited control over student learning in the school." This finding is noteworthy because it suggests that majorities of principals support the idea that principals are responsible for student learning. However, majorities of principals in year 4, as in previous years, expressed concerns about the fairness of the measure used to award bonuses, and only 10 percent expressed the opinion that the bonus measure did a good job of distinguishing effective from ineffective principals. None of the principals who participated in the interviews expressed positive views of the bonus; most said that they believed that the bonus favored schools unlike their own (when, in fact, the bonus did not favor any particular type of school). These findings suggest a need for continued communication regarding the features and goals of the bonus measure. Moreover, more than two-thirds of year 4 principal survey respondents reported no effect of the bonus on their practices, and interview participants indicated that the prospect of earning additional money was not a motivator.

The premium for working in high-need schools did not appear to affect principals' decisions about where to work. Approximately half of principals who responded to the survey in year 4 indicated awareness of the high-need school premium. Of these principals who knew about the high-need premium, only one in five agreed that it provided an adequate incentive for principals to work in high-need schools. The district's efforts to use the premium as a means of luring effective principals to the neediest schools may be hindered by a lack of awareness and a lack of enthusiasm on the part of principals. However, as we discussed in Chapter Six, we found that the principals who moved to higher-need schools had higher prior achievement bonuses than those who moved to lower-need schools. This could reflect the district's reassignment of principals who have overseen achievement gains to high-need schools, or it could reflect a desire to work in high-need schools by effective principals who were aware of the premium.

In What Ways Did Principals' Skills and Practices Change over the Course of the Pittsburgh Principal Incentive Program?

Over the course of PPIP implementation, principals reported spending increasing amounts of time observing teachers and providing feedback on their instruction and reported that these were the areas in which their skills grew the most. The changes in the rubric-based evaluation process were intended to promote a focus on the principal's role as instructional leader. These changes were supported by the district's professional development, particularly the Leadership Academy, and by coaching from their assistant superintendents. Principals reported spending more time in classrooms since the implementation of PPIP, and coaches who responded to the coach survey corroborated these reports of increased principal presence in classrooms. Coaches also reported that teachers in their schools found principals' feedback useful and that principals were effective in the areas of providing professional development opportunities, giving feedback on instruction, and helping teachers use data. Additional supporting evidence was obtained from a teacher survey in the last year of the evaluation, on which large majorities of teachers rated their principals highly as instructional leaders. Moreover, when principal survey respondents were asked to select areas in which their skills had grown the most since PPIP implementation, the most–frequently selected skills were (1) observing in teachers' classrooms and providing feedback and (2) evaluating teachers. At the same time, principals mentioned other areas of instructional leadership, including curriculum implementation and data use, as areas in which they would like the district to provide additional training and support.

Some principals attributed changes in their practice to RISE rather than to PPIP. The wide variety of reforms taking place in PPS made it impossible to attribute any changes directly to PPIP, and this problem of attribution was made more challenging by the fact that the district explicitly tried to ensure that its multiple reforms worked together seamlessly. This coherence among reform efforts is likely beneficial for promoting the desired changes, and the data we collected from principals suggest that principals were hearing the message of a unified approach to reform. In particular, throughout the evaluation, principals who participated in interviews were reluctant to attribute changes in their practice to PPIP, especially to the financial incentives. Principals who participated in interviews in year 4 tended to associate changes in their practice with the requirements of RISE, but they also noted that RISE and PPIP reinforced one another, and it is possible that PPIP created conditions that led to greater acceptance of RISE than what would have occurred in the absence of PPIP.

What Conditions Changed at the School and Classroom Levels over the Course of the Pittsburgh Principal Incentive Program?

During PPIP implementation, principals became more-active data users and provided support and structures for increased instructional data use by their teaching staff. The interview data collected over the course of this evaluation indicate that school-level data use became more frequent, more consistent, and more in-depth, with staff using a greater variety of data sources and drilling down into more-detailed data (e.g., to individual students, groups of students, and content standards). In years 3 and 4, principals and other school staff who participated in interviews noted that the increased data use at the school level had resulted in students becoming more aware of their own performance, which respondents viewed as beneficial. Principal interview participants in year 4 were more likely than those in year 3 to describe data being used to design and target interventions. At the same time, the year 4 surveys suggest a decline in agreement among principals and coaches that their teachers not only have the skills and knowledge to use data effectively but are also regularly using data for instructional decision making. This perceived decline could reflect principals' greater awareness of teachers' skills and practices, stemming from principals' increased role as coaches and evaluators of teachers.

Principals and coaches reported classroom-level evidence of the major instructional improvement strategies used under PPIP: principal feedback, site-specific professional development, and instructional data use. Majorities of principals and coaches reported seeing specific evidence that three major instructional improvement strategies—principal feedback, site-specific professional development, and data work—were used in the classroom. In addition, principal/coach pairs who participated in interviews in year 4 described improvements in teaching that included improved questioning techniques, more-effective data use, more-rigorous classroom discussions, and increased collaboration among teachers around instruction. Principals and coaches also described increased levels of student engagement—specifically, that students were taking ownership of their own learning. As with the changes to principals' practices and skills, all of these school-level changes were supported by multiple strands of the district's improvement strategy, making direct attribution to PPIP impossible, and other initiatives clearly made important contributions. In particular, year 4 principal interview participants saw RISE as actively accelerating the goals of PPIP by giving principals more-concrete tools to meet broad initiative goals.

How Did Principals Perform on the Rubric and Bonus Measures, and How Was Performance Related to Principal Mobility?

Average principal performance on the rubric has remained steady over time, with principals performing most poorly on the standard related to creating a culture of teaching and learning. The distribution of scores on the rubric remained relatively consistent over the course of PPIP implementation, and, in each of the years during which rubric data were collected, the lowest scores were observed on the standard measuring principals' skill at creating a culture of teaching and learning, which includes such activities as data use, curriculum implementation, and differentiated instruction. The scores on the individual standards and components were correlated, and the rubric appeared to measure a single construct related to principal leadership. We observed some differences in rubric performance across school types and across schools serving students with different characteristics, although the exact nature of these differences has varied from year to year.

Performance on the bonus measure has been relatively constant over time, and no consistent relationships with student characteristics were observed. This stability in average performance on the bonus measure suggests that an achievement bonus program can be designed so that bonuses change to reflect changes in achievement growth but do not change so much as to create the risk of an overwhelming unanticipated financial burden. And the lack of relationships with student characteristics provides some assurance that principals' concerns about lack of fairness are unwarranted.

There is some evidence that the skills and practices measured by the rubric are associated with improved student achievement. In year 4, mathematics achievement growth showed a statistically significant positive correlation with the first three rubric standards and with the total score. In earlier years, there was evidence of a positive correlation between growth in rubric scores and subsequent achievement growth. Together, these findings provide some evidence that the rubric is working as a measure of practices and skills that are associated with principal effectiveness. This relationship is foundational to any program that is trying to increase student achievement by evaluating and improving principals' practice and should be continually monitored.

Principal mobility has remained fairly constant, and the association with average bonus, although in the expected direction, is not statistically significant. The percentage of principals who remained at their schools stayed fairly constant throughout the program, though retirements declined somewhat over time. Although we did not find significant differences in prior achievement bonuses by move type (e.g., whether the principal left the district, switched schools, retired), the patterns were suggestive. For example, principals who moved into administrative positions at the central office level had higher-than-average achievement bonuses prior to their move than other principals, and those who moved from a principal to an assistant principal position had lower bonuses. This finding is consistent with the hypothesis that high-performing principals would be likely to receive promotions whereas low-performing principals would be counseled into positions that would offer them additional experience to improve their practices. Principals who left the district without retiring had slightly lower achievement than the overall average, a pattern that, if it continues, will eventually lead to an increase in the average performance of principals in PPS.

Principals who move to higher-need schools had earned higher bonuses than other principals before the move, but high-need schools experienced greater principal turnover than other schools. We found a strong association between the achievement bonus amount known at the time of a principal's reassignment and whether a principal moved to a principal position in a higher-need school. Principals who moved to higher-need schools earned approximately $1,900 more in bonus in the first year of the two-year average than principals who moved to lower-need schools. This finding is consistent with the intention of the district to place higher-performing principals in high-need schools. In addition, turnover was high among principals at high-need schools; schools in the most disadvantaged quartile had a 43-percent annual turnover rate, which was 23 percentage points higher than in other schools. Of course, high levels of turnover may or may not be considered problematic; if the departing principals are replaced by more-effective leaders, turnover could be desirable, at least in the early stages of a reform like PPIP.

How Did Student Achievement Change During the Course of the Pittsburgh Principal Incentive Program, and How Did Racial and Socioeconomic Gaps Change?

The district experienced positive achievement growth during the time PPIP was implemented, particularly in the final year. Student achievement growth in grades 4–8 in both mathematics and reading reached their highest levels since the beginning of our evaluation, and growth surpassed that of the rest of the state in three out of four years since the beginning of PPIP. This finding suggests that the implementation of PPIP was accompanied by acceleration in achievement growth, consistent with the district's goal of promoting more-effective school leadership as a means of improving student achievement. At the same time, scores on the third-grade reading emphasis measure experienced no growth and even a small decline in year 4. We also found that achievement growth estimated from a low-stakes early elementary reading test (DIBELS) yielded conclusions about growth that were similar to what we found when using the higher-stakes SPI-2 measures.

Race and poverty achievement gaps increased over the course of PPIP implementation by some measures. PPIP was designed in part to reduce achievement gaps between racial/ethnic groups and between high- and low-income students. Although the state testing system emphasizes the use of the percentage-proficient-or-above metric for reporting on student achievement, we investigated gaps using scale scores for continuing students rather than proficiency rates for all students in order to measure actual growth throughout the range of achievement and to reduce distortion stemming from differences in the cohorts of students included each year. When measured in this way, race and poverty gaps increased every year since before PPIP was implemented.

There is suggestive evidence that achievement growth among the lowest-scoring students and at the most-disadvantaged schools is increasing. Although achievement gaps for continuing students grew, we find direct evidence that PPIP worked to make these gaps grow less than they otherwise would have. Our analyses indicate that, in year 4, previously low-scoring students experienced greater achievement growth than in prior years, which is consistent with a design feature of the bonus formula (i.e., the focus on measuring percentage growth, which rewards gains at the low end of the distribution more than comparable gains at the high end). Furthermore, we found evidence that achievement growth in high-need schools increased following the implementation of the high-need bonus premium, suggesting that the premium may be promoting increased achievement growth at the most-disadvantaged schools. These findings suggest that PPIP can be an important part of continued efforts to reduce the achievement gap.

Recommendations

Because the evaluation design does not permit strong causal conclusions regarding the effects of performance-based evaluation and compensation for principals, our findings do not support recommendations regarding whether or not districts or states should adopt such policies. Nonetheless, as PPS continues to advance its ambitious reform agenda, the findings from this evaluation can be used to develop guidance to inform the district's efforts to maintain a focus on developing, supporting, and incentivizing effective school leadership in the context of the broader set of initiatives. Our findings could also be informative to districts, states, charter management organizations, or other education agencies that are developing new principal evaluation and compensation systems, although, for simplicity, we refer only to districts in most of the discussion that follows. In this final section, we list several recommendations that PPS and other entities might consider as they develop or revise principal evaluation, support, and compensation policies. We first present recommendations related to the development and refinement of evaluation systems, and we then discuss ideas related to the implementation of these systems.

Recommendations for Evaluation System and Measure Development

Consider incorporating a range of measures into the evaluation system, including measures that reflect input from a variety of stakeholders. The surveys and case studies we conducted enabled us to collect information about school leadership not only from the principals who provide that leadership but also from other staff in the building who work with the principals. The views expressed by teachers and coaches often serve as a means of corroborating principals' self-reports, but they also sometimes provide a different perspective. This type of feedback, if collected regularly and systematically, could help principals assess the extent to which their instructional improvement efforts are leading to the desired effects on school staff, and it could enable principals to pinpoint areas for improvement. Information from other stakeholders, such as parents and students, could also prove helpful for understanding principals' performance. These data could be collected in a variety of ways, but, for the purposes of formal evaluation, it should be done consistently across schools and ideally in a way that permits quantification of the information. The VAL-ED principal evaluation system provides one example of how multiple stakeholder groups can be involved in principal evaluation (see VAL-ED, undated), and many districts already administer instruments, such as teacher working conditions surveys, that could be incorporated into the system. It is critical that any measure used for the purpose of evaluating principals be carefully piloted and subject to an investigation of the validity of that measure for that specific purpose; instruments that work well for providing formative feedback, for instance, could provide misleading information or be subject to score corruption if used for high-stakes evaluation purposes.

Gather evidence of validity, reliability, and fairness of the system throughout the implementation of the system, not just at the beginning. The changes we observed in the correlations between the bonus and rubric measures provide an example of how the characteristics of scores can change over time. Districts should continually gather evidence to identify changes in rater agreement, relationships among measures, relationships with external criteria, and fairness to all participants. The *Standards for Educational and Psychological Testing* provide a useful summary of the types of evidence that can support validity and reliability investigations (AERA, APA, and NCME, 1999), and the Porter et al. (2010) analysis of the VAL-ED is a helpful illustrative example of how to carry out these investigations. Any problems that are identified should be quickly addressed to ensure that the system continues to function effectively. Changes to the evaluation system might also be warranted as the needs and emphases of states or districts are modified, necessitating changes in how principals carry out their work. Alignment of the system with broader district or state goals should be a focus of these ongoing investigations.

Take steps to ensure consistency in application of rubrics across evaluators. For principals to support an evaluation system, it is important to convince them that the method used to assign ratings is fair to all principals, regardless of what type of school they lead or who their evaluator happens to be. The concerns about consistency that we heard from principals throughout implementation of PPIP could undermine their support for the program. Although traditional methods for measuring interrater agreement are difficult to apply in PPIP because each assistant superintendent works with only one type of school, there are several approaches to improving consistency that could be helpful. These include calibration meetings at which the evaluators rate evidence (either from an actual principal or from a set of mock documents) and discuss their criteria in an effort to promote consensus, comparisons of the distributions of scores produced by each evaluator to help them identify the extent to which their ratings differ in magnitude or in variability, and a careful examination of the narrative comments that evaluators produce, which can serve as a means of identifying and addressing differences in what factors each one pays attention to and how they translate these narrative impressions into scores. It could also be helpful to examine the predictive power of both between- and within-rater variation on rubric scores for predicting achievement in subsequent years, as a means of understanding the extent to which assistant superintendents are applying different standards. The analysis can also identify evaluators whose ratings are not associated with future student achievement, thus precipitating further investigation of the reasons for the lack of relationships. Regardless of which approach is taken, the district or state adopting the evaluation system should let principals know that it is taking steps to improve consistency of rubric application and should assure principals that their concerns are being addressed. Those who supervise principals should also receive professional development to help them provide more-effective support to principals based on their performance on the evaluation system.

On measures of principal practice, develop a scale that differentiates performance at all points along the distribution. Because the vast majority of scores assigned to principals on the PPIP rubric have been 3s and 4s, the four-point rating scale offers little opportunity to distinguish between the most-outstanding principals and those who are performing well but not at the highest level. Developing a more expansive rating scale that permits fine-grained distinctions at the high end of the distribution could help districts and states ensure that they are encouraging and rewarding the most-effective principals, and it could provide information that is useful for identifying principals who could serve in mentoring roles. It could also support targeted professional development for principals. If programs, such as PPIP, have their intended effects, we would expect to see improvements over time in principal performance on these measures, which will exacerbate the problem of lack of variability at the high end of the scale. The development of an expanded scale should reflect the district's understanding of what it means to be a highly effective school leader. One option is to distinguish among high-performing principals by identifying those who not only perform well themselves but who also help promote the skills and knowledge of others with whom they work. Even one point added to the four-point scale would enable the district to make some of these distinctions. Those who evaluate principals could provide useful input for identifying ways in which the attributes and practices of the highest-performing principals with whom they work differ from those of the principals who perform well but somewhat less effectively. Of course, achieving high levels of rater consistency with an expanded scale will require additional training in the application of the scale, along with clear rating criteria.

Involve all stakeholders in any reviews and redesigns of measures used in evaluation systems. By definition, incentive pay systems designed to reward complex changes in behavior are complicated and often controversial. For example, systems that reward both overall achievement growth and reductions in achievement gaps will be more complex than systems that do only one or the other. Also, systems that try to prevent unintended consequences, such as focusing on students near the proficiency cutoff or focusing on tested grades and subjects, can be complex and unfamiliar. It is important that districts cultivate shared goals among stakeholders, such as parents, teachers, principals, and central office staff. Once shared goals are established, measures can be reviewed based on the stakeholders' ability to attain these goals.

Monitor racial and socioeconomic achievement gaps using student-level growth throughout the achievement distribution. Given the importance that many districts have placed on the goal of reducing achievement gaps, it would be worthwhile to monitor progress toward this goal using multiple metrics. The practice of tracking changes in percentage proficient across cohorts provides useful information, but it may lead to distorted impressions regarding the nature and extent of improvement among individual students who are performing at different points in the achievement distribution. By also examining student-level growth in scale scores for students who remain in the district for at least two consecutive years, the district can provide richer and more-accurate information to inform its own decision making and to enhance public understanding of the district's progress. Furthermore, differences between the changes in gaps for continuing students and changes between cohorts can provide useful insight into the characteristics of students who are entering or leaving the district.

Recommendations for Implementation

Align the elements of a performance-based compensation system, including support and criteria for evaluation, with the district's approach to improving teaching and learning. One of the messages that PPS sent, and that principals and other school staff reported hearing, is that the multitude of reforms the district had undertaken were intended to work coherently and toward the common goals of improving teaching and learning and student achievement throughout the district. Principals' generally high level of satisfaction with the changes to the rubric in year 4, and with the alignment of PPIP and RISE more generally, suggest that principals perceived these reforms as reinforcing one another. Educators who are participating in these kinds of ambitious reforms are more likely to support the reforms and respond effectively when the reforms do not conflict with one another and when they can clearly see the connections among them. The alignment among the rubric criteria; the professional development principals received; other ongoing reforms, such as RISE; and the support from other sources appeared to be critical factors in promoting the district's intended outcomes. Districts or states undertaking similar reforms should consider the extent to which evaluation criteria, professional development, and other elements of the reform support or conflict with other key initiatives.

Devise a communication strategy that provides clear, timely, and ongoing information to help principals understand the evaluation measures and the steps the district took to ensure their validity. Principals expressed significant concerns about both the bonus and rubric measures throughout the course of the evaluation. Although opinions improved in some areas, majorities of principals continued to doubt the validity and fairness of the measures, particularly the bonus measure. Moreover, many of the principals in the PPIP evaluation were unaware of specific features of the incentive pay that were designed to reward principals who reduced achievement gaps, and this lack of awareness could limit the extent to which the PPIP incentives worked in the way the district had hoped. These perceptions and lack of understanding are certainly not unique to PPIP, and they suggest that any effort by a district or other entity to adopt performance-based compensation should be accompanied not only by efforts to establish the validity and reliability of the measures but also by a communication strategy that provides clear, timely, and ongoing information to stakeholders. Although some of the objections that principals raised reflect a deep-seated resistance to pay for performance and will not be easily altered, the improvement on some dimensions that we observed over time suggests that principals' opinions can be shaped by their experiences and understanding of the program. A comprehensive communication strategy should involve multiple vehicles of information dissemination, including large-group meetings, as well as individualized interactions and stakeholder involvement in decisions about changes to the program. Principals' supervisors can play an important role, especially in light of concerns about specific components of the bonus measure that might be relevant to particular types of schools (e.g., the third-grade reading measure and the high school measures). In explaining and promoting incentive-based compensation, those responsible for adopting performance-based pay should recognize that the culture of K–12 education does not encourage people to admit they are motivated by money, so it is important to present the performance-based compensation policies as one part of a much broader strategy to build capacity.

Provide principals with concrete tools for accomplishing the instructional leadership tasks (especially observing and providing feedback on instruction) encouraged by the compensation system. PPIP, like many evaluation systems, was designed to support improvement, which is likely to require not only feedback but also resources to help principals improve their knowledge and practices. We found that principals perceived resources, such as professional development that was aligned with the goals of the program, targeted support from supervisors, and a clear set of standards communicated by the rubric, as contributing to their professional growth. The positive perceptions about the utility of the DPG projects suggest that this type of activity could be a valuable tool, particularly for helping more-experienced and accomplished principals enhance their knowledge and skills in a particular area.

Help principals find the time needed to engage in the practices promoted by the initiative. If the initiative encourages principals to spend more time on specific tasks, such as supporting teachers, it is important to help them find that time. Districts could encourage discussion of tasks principals might spend less time on and the most-effective ways to incorporate delegation in their leadership approach. Districts could also create structures that facilitate delegation. This might be challenging in districts facing budget reductions, which might be under pressure to reduce administrative staff time at the school and central office levels, but it should be possible to think creatively about how to involve existing school staff in ways that allow principals to focus on the most-important practices. In fact, the ability to cultivate leadership among school staff is an important element of effective leadership and could be directly incorporated into the evaluation and support systems, particularly for experienced principals.

Assess the extent to which principal mobility leads to improved access to effective principals at high-need schools and to higher levels of principal effectiveness overall. We found that high-need schools experienced greater principal mobility than other schools and that principals who switched schools and moved to higher-need schools had higher prior performance on the bonus measure than those who moved to lower-need schools. It is not clear whether the higher mobility levels in high-need schools will lead to disruption or to improved educational quality, so districts and states should monitor mobility over time to determine whether equity and overall effectiveness are improving. It would also be helpful to assess whether principal promotions into central office positions negatively affect student learning in some instances by taking the most-effective leaders out of the schools.

Conclusion

PPS undertook an ambitious set of reforms when it implemented PPIP, and the district's experiences can be informative for other efforts to adopt performance-based evaluation and compensation programs for principals. The recommendations presented in this section are unlikely to apply uniformly to all districts, states, or other agencies that are implementing these systems, but the lessons learned through this evaluation can provide a starting point and guidance for ongoing efforts to promote high-quality evaluation policies and practices and to monitor the system's effects on teaching and learning.

References

AERA, APA, and NCME—*See* American Educational Research Association, American Psychological Association, and National Council on Measurement in Education.

American Educational Research Association, American Psychological Association, and National Council on Measurement in Education, *Standards for Educational and Psychological Testing*, Washington, D.C., 1999.

Augustine, Catherine H., Gabriella C. Gonzalez, Gina Schuyler Ikemoto, Jennifer Russell, Gail L. Zellman, Louay Constant, Jane Armstrong, and Jacob W. Dembosky, *Improving School Leadership: The Promise of Cohesive Leadership Systems*, Santa Monica, Calif.: RAND Corporation, MG-885-WF, 2009. As of April 25, 2012:
http://www.rand.org/pubs/monographs/MG885.html

Beteille, Tara, Demetra Kalogrides, and Susanna Loeb, *Effective Schools: Managing the Recruitment, Development, and Retention of High-Quality Teachers*, Washington, D.C.: Urban Institute, December 15, 2009. As of April 25, 2012:
http://www.urban.org/publications/1001428.html

Birckmayer, Johanna D., and Carol H. Weiss, "Theory-Based Evaluation in Practice: What Do We Learn?" *Evaluation Review*, Vol. 24, No. 4, August 2000, pp. 407–431.

Branch, Gregory F., Eric A. Hanushek, and Steven G. Rivkin, *Estimating the Effect of Leaders on Public Sector Productivity: The Case of School Principals*, Cambridge, Mass.: National Bureau of Economic Research, Working Paper 17803, February 2012. As of April 25, 2012:
http://papers.nber.org/papers/17803

Burkhauser, Susan, Susan M. Gates, Laura S. Hamilton, and Gina Schuyler Ikemoto, *First-Year Principals in Urban School Districts: How Actions and Working Conditions Relate to Outcomes*, Santa Monica, Calif.: RAND Corporation, TR-1191-NLNS, 2012. As of April 25, 2012:
http://www.rand.org/pubs/technical_reports/TR1191.html

Center on Education Policy, *Answering the Question That Matters Most: Has Student Achievement Increased Since No Child Left Behind?* Washington, D.C., June 2007. As of May 16, 2012:
http://www.cep-dc.org/
cfcontent_file.cfm?Attachment=CEP_Report_StudentAchievement_053107.pdf

Clark, Damon, Paco Martorell, and Jonah E. Rockoff, *School Principals and School Performance*, Washington, D.C.: Urban Institute, National Center for Analysis of Longitudinal Data in Education Research Working Paper 38, December 2009. As of April 25, 2012:
http://www.urban.org/UploadedPDF/1001427-school-principals.pdf

Coelli, Michael, and David A. Green, "Leadership Effects: School Principals and Student Outcomes," *Economics of Education Review*, Vol. 31, No. 1, February 2012, pp. 92–109.

Council of Chief State School Officers, *Educational Leadership Policy Standards: ISLLC 2008—as Adopted by the National Policy Board for Educational Administration*, Washington, D.C., 2008. As of May 16, 2012:
http://www.ccsso.org/Documents/2008/Educational_Leadership_Policy_Standards_2008.pdf

Cuban, Larry, *The Managerial Imperative and the Practice of Leadership in Schools*, Albany, N.Y.: State University of New York Press, 1988.

Darling-Hammond, Linda, Michelle LaPointe, Debra Meyerson, Margaret Terry Orr, and Carol Cohen, *Preparing School Leaders for a Changing World: Lessons from Exemplary Leadership Development Programs*, Stanford, Calif.: Stanford Educational Leadership Institute, Stanford University, 2007.

Davis, Stephen, Linda Darling-Hammond, Michelle LaPointe, and Debra Meyerson, *School Leadership Study: Developing Successful Principals*, Review of Research, Stanford, Calif.: Stanford University, Stanford Educational Leadership Institute, 2005. As of April 25, 2012:
http://seli.stanford.edu/research/documents/SELI_sls_research_review.pdf

Davis, Stephen H., Karen Kearney, Nancy M. Sanders, Christopher N. Thomas, and Ronald J. Leon, *The Policies and Practices of Principal Evaluation: A Review of the Literature*, San Francisco, Calif.: WestEd, 2011. As of February 17, 2012:
http://www.wested.org/online_pubs/resource1104.pdf

Derrington, Mary Lynne, and Kellie Sanders, "Conceptualizing a System for Principal Evaluation," *AASA Journal of Scholarship and Research*, Vol. 7, No. 4, Winter 2011, pp. 32–38.

Focus on Results, undated home page. As of April 30, 2012:
http://www.focusonresults.net/

Fullan, Michael, *The Development of Transformational Leaders for Educational Decentralization*, Toronto, Ont., 2006.

Fuller, Ed, Michelle Young, and Bruce D. Baker, "Do Principal Preparation Programs Influence Student Achievement Through the Building of Teacher-Team Qualifications by the Principal? An Exploratory Analysis," *Educational Administration Quarterly*, Vol. 47, No. 1, February 2011, pp. 173–216.

Gill, Brian, John Engberg, and Kevin Booker, *Assessing the Performance of Public Schools in Pittsburgh*, Santa Monica, Calif.: RAND Corporation, WR-315-1-EDU, 2005. As of February 27, 2012:
http://www.rand.org/pubs/working_papers/WR315-1.html

Goldring, Ellen, Xiu Chen Cravens, Joseph Murphy, Andrew C. Porter, Stephen N. Elliott, and Becca Carson, "The Evaluation of Principals: What and How Do States and Urban Districts Assess Leadership?" *Elementary School Journal*, Vol. 110, No. 1, September 2009, pp. 19–39.

Gonzalez, Gabriella C., Robert Bozick, Shannah Tharp-Taylor, and Andrea Phillips, *Fulfilling the Pittsburgh Promise®: Early Progress of Pittsburgh's Postsecondary Scholarship Program*, Santa Monica, Calif.: RAND Corporation, MG-1139-TPP, 2011. As of February 8, 2012:
http://www.rand.org/pubs/monographs/MG1139.html

Grissom, Jason A., and Susanna Loeb, "Triangulating Principal Effectiveness: How Perspectives of Parents, Teachers, and Assistant Principals Identify the Central Importance of Managerial Skills," Washington, D.C.: Urban Institute, December 1, 2009. As of April 25, 2012:
http://www.urban.org/publications/1001443.html

Hallinger, Philip, "Instructional Leadership and the School Principal: A Passing Fancy That Refuses to Fade Away," *Leadership and Policy in Schools*, Vol. 4, No. 3, September 2005, pp. 221–239.

Hallinger, Philip, Leonard Bickman, and Ken Davis, "School Context, Principal Leadership, and Student Reading Achievement," *Elementary School Journal*, Vol. 96, No. 5, May 1996, pp. 527–549.

Hallinger, Philip, and Ronald H. Heck, "Reassessing the Principal's Role in School Effectiveness: A Review of Empirical Research, 1980–1995," *Educational Administration Quarterly*, Vol. 32, No. 1, February 1996, pp. 5–44.

Hallinger, Philip, and Joseph Murphy, "Assessing the Instructional Management Behavior of Principals," *Elementary School Journal*, Vol. 86, No. 2, November 1985, pp. 217–248.

Halverson, Richard, *School Leadership Rubrics, System-Wide Change for All Learners and Educators (SCALE)*, Madison, Wis.: University of Wisconsin–Madison, Wisconsin Center for Education Research, 2005.

Heck, Ronald H., and Philip Hallinger, "Assessing the Contribution of Distributed Leadership to School Improvement and Growth in Math Achievement," *American Educational Research Journal*, Vol. 46, No. 3, September 2009, pp. 659–689.

Horng, Eileen Lai, Demetra Kalogrides, and Susanna Loeb, *Principal Preferences and the Unequal Distribution of Principals Across Schools*, Washington, D.C.: Urban Institute, December 1, 2009. As of April 25, 2012:
http://www.urban.org/publications/1001442.html

Horng, Eileen Lai, Daniel Klasik, and Susanna Loeb, "Principal's Time Use and School Effectiveness," *American Journal of Education*, Vol. 116, No. 4, 2010, pp. 491–523.

Kimball, Steven Miller, Anthony Milanowski, and Sarah A. McKinney, "Assessing the Promise of Standards-Based Performance Evaluation for Principals: Results from a Randomized Trial," *Leadership and Policy in Schools*, Vol. 8, No. 3, 2009, pp. 233–263.

Knapp, Michael S., Michael A. Copland, Brynnen Ford, Anneke Markholt, Milbrey W. McLaughlin, Michael Milliken, and Joan E. Talbert, *Leading for Learning Sourcebook: Concepts and Examples*, Seattle, Wash.: Center for the Study of Teaching and Policy, University of Washington, February 2003. As of February 20, 2012:
http://depts.washington.edu/ctpmail/PDFs/LforLSourcebook-02-03.pdf

Knapp, Michael S., Michael A. Copland, and Joan E. Talbert, *Leading for Learning: Reflective Tools for School and District Leaders*, Seattle, Wash.: Center for the Study of Teaching and Policy, University of Washington, February 2003. As of February 20, 2012:
http://depts.washington.edu/ctpmail/PDFs/LforLSummary-02-03.pdf

Lachat, Mary Ann, and Stephen Smith, "Practices That Support Data Use in Urban High Schools," *Journal of Education for Students Placed at Risk*, Vol. 10, No. 3, 2005, pp. 333–349.

Ladd, Helen F., *Teachers' Perceptions of Their Working Conditions: How Predictive of Policy-Relevant Outcomes?* Washington, D.C.: Urban Institute, National Center for Analysis of Longitudinal Data in Education Research Working Paper 33, December 2009. As of April 25, 2012:
http://www.urban.org/UploadedPDF/1001440-Teachers-Perceptions.pdf

Leithwood, Kenneth A., Karen Seashore Louis, Stephen Anderson, and Kyla Wahlstrom, *How Leadership Influences Student Learning*, Minneapolis, Minn.: Center for Applied Research and Educational Improvement, University of Minnesota, September 2004.

Lipscomb, Stephen, Bing-ru Teh, Brian Gill, Hanley Chiang, and Antoniya Owens, *Teacher and Principal Value-Added: Research Findings and Implementation Practices*, Cambridge, Mass: Mathematica Policy Research, September 14, 2010. As of February 20, 2012:
http://www.mathematica-mpr.com/publications/PDFs/education/teacherprin_valueadded.pdf

Louis, Karen Seashore, Kenneth Leithwood, Kyla L. Wahlstrom, and Stephen E. Anderson, *Investigating the Links to Improved Student Learning: Final Report of Research Findings*, Minneapolis, Minn.: University of Minnesota, 2010. As of January 9, 2012:
http://www.wallacefoundation.org/knowledge-center/school-leadership/key-research/Documents/Investigating-the-Links-to-Improved-Student-Learning.pdf

Marsh, Julie A., Matthew G. Springer, Daniel F. McCaffrey, Kun Yuan, Scott Epstein, Julia Koppich, Nidhi Kalra, Catherine DiMartino, and Art (Xiao) Peng, *A Big Apple for Educators: New York City's Experiment with Schoolwide Performance Bonuses*, Santa Monica, Calif.: RAND Corporation, MG-1114-FPS, 2011. As of April 25, 2012:
http://www.rand.org/pubs/monographs/MG1114.html

Marzano, Robert J., Timothy Waters, and Brian A. McNulty, *School Leadership That Works: From Research to Results*, Denver, Colo.: Mid-Continent Research for Education and Learning, 2005. As of January 23, 2012:
http://www.ascd.org/publications/books/105125.aspx

McCaffrey, Daniel F., Tim R. Sass, J. R. Lockwood, and Kata Mihaly, "The Intertemporal Variability of Teacher Effect Estimates," *Education Finance and Policy*, Vol. 4, No. 4, Fall 2009, pp. 572–606.

Pearson, "School Improvement Services," undated. As of April 27, 2012:
http://www.americaschoice.org/

Pennsylvania Department of Education, "Assessment," undated.

Peterson, Kent D., "The Professional Development of Principals: Innovations and Opportunities," in Michelle D. Young, ed., *Ensuring the University's Capacity to Prepare Learning-Focused Leadership*, Columbia, Mo.: National Commission for the Advancement of Educational Leadership Preparation, 2002.

Pittsburgh Public Schools, "Accelerated Learning Academies (ALAs)," undated (a). As of April 30, 2012:
http://www.pps.k12.pa.us/1431107251091897/site/default.asp?14311071716911330Nav=|&NodeID=5369

———, "Excel.9–12: The Plan for High School Excellence," undated (b). As of April 30, 2012:
http://www.pps.k12.pa.us/14311051715526407/site/default.asp?

———, "Excellence for All Reform Agenda," undated (c).

———, "Board of Education Approves the Superintendent's Right-Sizing Plan," press release, February 28, 2006. As of April 30, 2012:
http://www.pps.k12.pa.us/14311071716911330/lib/14311071716911330/rspnr2-28-06.pdf

———, *Empowering Effective Teachers in the Pittsburgh Public Schools*, 2009.

———, *Your Guide to Offerings and Options in the Pittsburgh Public Schools 2010–2011*, c. 2010.

Porter, Andrew C., Morgan S. Polikoff, Ellen B. Goldring, Joseph Murphy, Stephen N. Elliott, and Henry May, "Investigating the Validity and Reliability of the Vanderbilt Assessment of Leadership in Education," *Elementary School Journal*, Vol. 111, No. 2, 2010, pp. 282–313.

Portin, Bradley, Paul Schneider, Michael DeArmond, and Lauren Gundlach, *Making Sense of Leading Schools: A Study of the School Principalship*, Seattle, Wash.: Center on Reinventing Public Education, University of Washington, September 2003. As of October 18, 2009:
http://www.crpe.org/cs/crpe/view/csr_pubs/24

PPS—*See* Pittsburgh Public Schools.

Rice, Jennifer King, *Principal Effectiveness and Leadership in an Era of Accountability: What Research Says*, Washington, D.C.: Urban Institute, April 23, 2010. As of April 25, 2012:
http://www.urban.org/publications/1001370.html

Robinson, Viviane M. J., Claire A. Lloyd, and Kenneth J. Rowe, "The Impact of Leadership on Student Outcomes: An Analysis of the Differential Effects of Leadership Types," *Education Administration Quarterly*, Vol. 44, No. 5, December 2008, pp. 635–674.

Springer, Matthew G., Dale Ballou, Laura Hamilton, Vi-Nhuan Le, J. R. Lockwood, Daniel F. McCaffrey, Matthew Pepper, and Brian M. Stecher, *Teacher Pay for Performance: Experimental Evidence from the Project on Incentives in Teaching*, Nashville, Tenn.: National Center on Performance Incentives, Vanderbilt University, September 21, 2010. As of April 25, 2012:
http://www.rand.org/pubs/reprints/RP1416.html

Springer, Matthew G., John Pane, Vi-Nhuan Le, Daniel F. McCaffrey, S. Burns, Laura Hamilton, and Brian M. Stecher, "Team Pay for Performance: Experimental Evidence from the Round Rock Pilot Project on Team Incentives," *Educational Evaluation and Policy Analysis*, forthcoming.

Stufflebeam, Daniel L., "A Depth Study of the Evaluation Requirement," *Theory into Practice*, Vol. 5, No. 3, June 1966, pp. 121–133.

———, "The CIPP Model for Evaluation," in Daniel L. Stufflebeam, George F. Madaus, and Thomas Kellaghan, eds., *Evaluation Models: Viewpoints on Educational and Human Services Evaluation*, 2nd ed., Boston, Mass.: Kluwer Academic Publishers, 2000, pp. 279–318.

Sun, Min, and Peter Youngs, "How Does District Principal Evaluation Affect Learning-Centered Principal Leadership? Evidence from Michigan School Districts," *Leadership and Policy in Schools*, Vol. 8, No. 4, 2009, pp. 411–445.

Supovitz, Jonathan, Philip Sirinides, and Henry May, "How Principals and Peers Influence Teaching and Learning," *Educational Administration Quarterly*, Vol. 46, No. 1, February 2010, pp. 31–56.

Tharp-Taylor, Shannah, Catherine Awsumb Nelson, Jacob W. Dembosky, and Brian Gill, *Partners in Pittsburgh Public Schools' Excellence for All Initiative: Findings from the First Year of Implementation*, Santa Monica, Calif.: RAND Corporation, DB-544-FFE, 2007. As of February 8, 2012:
http://www.rand.org/pubs/documented_briefings/DB544.html

Tharp-Taylor, Shannah, Catherine Awsumb Nelson, Laura S. Hamilton, and Kun Yuan, *Pittsburgh Public Schools' Excellence for All: Year 2 Evaluation*, Santa Monica, Calif.: RAND Corporation, DB-575-1-PPS, 2009. As of February 8, 2012:
http://www.rand.org/pubs/documented_briefings/DB575-1.html

VAL-ED—*See* Vanderbilt Assessment of Leadership in Education.

Vanderbilt Assessment of Leadership in Education, undated home page. As of May 2, 2012:
http://www.valed.com/

Wallace Foundation, *The School Principal as Leader: Guiding Schools to Better Teaching and Learning*, New York, January 2012. As of April 25, 2012:
http://bibpurl.oclc.org/web/45748

Waters, Tim, Robert J. Marzano, and Brian A. McNulty, *Balanced Leadership®: What 30 Years of Research Tells Us About the Effect of Leadership on Student Achievement*, Denver, Colo.: Mid-Continent Research for Education and Learning, 2003. As of April 25, 2012:
http://www.mcrel.org/products/144/

Weiss, Carol H. "How Can Theory-Based Evaluation Make Greater Headway?" *Evaluation Review*, Vol. 21, No. 4, August 1997, pp. 501–524.

West, Cathie E., and Mary Lynne Derrington, *Leadership Teaming: The Superintendent-Principal Relationship*, Thousand Oaks, Calif.: Corwin Press, 2009.

Young, Chris, "Making the Grade," *Pittsburgh City Paper*, August 30, 2007. As of April 30, 2012: http://www.pittsburghcitypaper.ws/pittsburgh/making-the-grade/Content?oid=1338973